# The Parables of

# Matthew 13

# The Parables of Matthew 13

Steve Lewis

*Bible Study Companion Series:*

# The Parables of Matthew 13

Steve Lewis

# Contents

# Reference Abbreviations

Barclay  William Barclay, *The Gospel of Matthew* Vol 2, (Westminster Press, 1975).

Benson  Jeffrey R. Benson, "The Kingdom Parables Of Matthew Thirteen," (*Central Bible Quarterly*, vol 22, Spring 1979).

Constable  Thomas Constable, *Notes on* Matthew (2023), https://planobiblechapel.org/tcon/notes/pdf/matthew.pdf

e-Sword  e-Sword Bible Study Software, https://e-Sword.net

France  R.T. France, *Gospel According to Matthew*, (Intervarsity Press, 1985).

Gaebelein  A.C. Gaebelein, *The Seven Parables*, (Bible House of Los Angeles (1906).

Glass  Ronald N. Glass, "The Parables of the Kingdom: A Paradigm for Consistent Dispensational Hermeneutics," (*Michigan Theological Journal*, Spring 1994).

Goebel  Siegfried Goebel, *The Parables Of Jesus: A Methodical Exposition*, (T&T Clark, 1883).

Grant  Frederick W. Grant, *The Mysteries of the Kingdom of Heaven*, https://www.stempublishing.com/authors/ FW_Grant/ FWG_Kingdom_Heaven.html

Hornock  Marcia Hornock, "Excavating The Parable Of The Sower: Discerning Jesus' Meaning," (*Journal of Dispensational Theology*, Sum 2015).

MacArthur  John MacArthur, *Matthew 8-15*, (Moody Publishers, 1987).

MBT  Lewis Sperry Chafer and John F. Walvoord, *Major Bible Themes*, (Zondervan, 1974).

McQuilkin  Robertson McQuilkin, *Understanding and Applying the Bible*, (Moody Press, 1992).

Middletown  Middletown Bible Church, *The Mysteries of the Kingdom*, https://www.middletownbiblechurch.org/ matthew/mat13.pdf

Moldenke  Harold N. Moldenke and Alma L. Moldenke, *Plants of the Bible*, (*Chronica Botanica*, 1952).

Morgan  G. Campbell Morgan, *The Parables of the Kingdom*, (Fleming H. Revell Company, 1907).

Mounce  William D. Mounce, *Dictionary of Old & New Testament Words*, (Zondervan, 2006).

Peters  George N.H. Peters, *The Theocratic Kingdom* (vol 2), (Funk & Wagnalls, 1884).

Pink  Arthur W. Pink, *The Prophetic Parables of Matthew 13* (1928), https://www.gracegems.org/Pink/ prophetic_parables_of_mat_13.htm

Stallard  Michael D. Stallard, "Hermeneutics and Matthew 13: Part II," (*Conservative Theological Journal*, Dec 2001).

Strauss  Lehman Strauss, *Prophetic Mysteries Revealed*, (Loizeaux Brothers, 1980).

Thomson  William M. Thomson, *Land and the Book*, (Harper & Brothers, 1882).

Toussaint-B  Stanley D. Toussaint, *Behold the King*, (Multnomah Press, 1980).

Toussaint-J  Stanley D. Toussaint, "The Introductory and Concluding Parables of Matthew Thirteen," (*Bibliotheca Sacra*, Oct-Dec 1964).

Walvoord  John F. Walvoord, *Every Prophecy of the Bible*, (David C. Cook, 2011).

Woods  Andrew M. Woods, *The Coming Kingdom*, (Grace Gospel Press, 2016).

Zuck  Roy B. Zuck, *Basic Bible Interpretation*, (Victor Books, 1991).

# Preface to the
# Bible Study Companion Series

Bible study is such an important activity because knowing and doing the will of God depends on an accurate understanding of His written Word. The obedient Christian life is based on the assumption that believers know the truth about what they are to obey. God has not been silent, and He has not left us without detailed instructions for living. We have God's complete revelation for us today in the Bible.

The Bible is a collection of writings that God directed and inspired men to write. It was recorded in the common languages that people used to communicate their ideas to each other. We must remember this as we study the Bible. The principles for Bible study follow the same rules we use every day to understand the meaning of any written communication.

As we study the Bible our goal should be to understand the message that the original text was intended to communicate. This means we are not allowed to make the Bible say what we want it to say. We must let the Bible speak for itself. The hard work of Bible study involves carefully examining the written text of Scripture in order to understand exactly what that text was intended to communicate.

Since the biblical authors used normal language, we must use the regular principles of grammar and sentence structure to understand the Bible's message. Scripture was not written in some secret code that requires a hidden formula to decipher. Instead it was written in the common languages of the people who lived during those times (Hebrew, Aramaic, and Greek). For that reason, this Bible Study Companion contains many references to the words, grammar, and sentence structure of the original languages. This is necessary because most of us are not familiar with the ways that ancient writers communicated, and these insights will help us to clearly understand their message.

We must also remember that the biblical writings were recorded at specific times in human history. They were written to specific readers in specific historical, geographical, and cultural situations. In order to understand the purpose and message of the Bible, we must also study the history, geography, and culture of the original writers and readers. The meaning of each biblical expression is influenced and even determined by the context in which it was written. As one scholar has said,

> Just as we may be puzzled by the way people do things in other countries, so we may be puzzled by what we read in the Bible. Therefore it is important to know what the people in the Bible thought, believed, said, did, and made. To the extent we do this we are able to comprehend it better and communicate it more accurately. If we fail to give attention to these matters of culture, then we may be guilty of reading into the Bible our own ideas. [Zuck, 79]

This Bible Study Companion will provide help as you go through the text of the Bible just as it was written, in a verse-by-verse manner. Since the original text was written and read in successive order, this companion guide will include definitions, concepts, and ideas that will help you to understand the meaning of the phrases and sentences in the order in which they unfold. It is our prayer that God will guide and direct your study of His Word so that you will experience the rich blessings that come from studying the Bible.

# Introduction to Matthew 13

## (Matthew 13:1-3)

The simple stories which Jesus spoke in Matthew 13 are quite well-known, even among people who do not believe that the Bible is the Word of God. Many people treat them the same way they would treat the fables of Aesop or the fairy tales of Hans Christian Andersen. But Jesus' parables in Matthew 13 are so much more than mere morality tales. The Lord was teaching important truths about the coming of His kingdom, as well as helping His disciples to understand their responsibilities during the time period between His first coming and His glorious return.

Our goal in this study will be to carefully examine the text to see exactly what Jesus says, and then to determine what message He wanted His disciples (and us) to understand from these important parables. As with any study of the Scriptures, one of the most important principles is to determine the context for the passage being examined. This is especially important when studying the parables of Matthew 13. With that in mind, let's begin our study of this chapter.

**Matt 13:1 - That day Jesus went out of the house and was sitting by the sea.**

The first two words of this verse immediately prompt us to ask, "Which day was that day?" In order to answer this question, we need to look back at the previous chapters in order to understand what had taken place.

Let's begin by briefly surveying what has happened so far in Matthew's narrative of the life of Jesus. In the first two chapters of Matthew we see His royal genealogy, remarkable birth, and His early life. In chapter 3 we see John the Baptist announcing the coming of the Messiah, baptizing Jesus in the Jordan River, and proclaiming, "Repent, for the kingdom of heaven is at hand" (Matt 3:2). But there was opposition to John's message and he was put in prison. Jesus then began His public ministry to the nation of Israel in chapter 4, where He taught in their synagogues, called His first disciples, miraculously healed many people, and proclaimed the same message which John the Baptist had declared: "Repent, for the kingdom of heaven is at hand" (Matt 4:17).

The kingdom being proclaimed was the same one that the Jewish people were already familiar with from the Old Testament Scriptures. They knew their history and they understood that God had brought the theocratic kingdom to an end, that God's shekinah glory had departed (Ezek 8:4; 9:3; 10:4; 11:22-23), and that God had judged His people by scattering them among the nations (Deut 28:64). The future restoration of the kingdom and the promised fulfillment of God's covenants with the nation of Israel was proclaimed by nearly every Old Testament prophet. This kingdom is the one that the Jews were anticipating and which Jesus declared was at hand. As one commentator has said,

> The promise of the kingdom could not be disassociated from the presence of the King. A kingdom demands a king. This was a well known fact which gave to Israel the confident expectation of their Messiah's coming. ... [Here] it was not that the kingdom had come, but rather that the King was present to offer His kingdom. [Strauss, 19, 21]

Notice that Jesus did not say, "The kingdom of heaven has been established." In essence His message was: "The King is here and it would be possible for Him to establish the kingdom if the nation of Israel would meet the condition for its

### Prophetic Promises of the Future Kingdom

- Isaiah 2:1-4; 4:2-6; 9:6-7; 11:1-13; 24:1-23; 32:1-5, 14-20; 33:17-24; 35:1-10; 40:1-11; 42:1-4; 52:7-10; 60:1-61:6; 65:17-25; 66:15-23
- Jeremiah 23:1-8; 31:1-37; 33:14-26
- Ezekiel 20:33-42; 34:20-31; 36:22-36; 37:1-28; 39:21-29; 43:1-7
- Daniel 2:31-45; 7:1-28; 9:1-3, 20-27; 12:1-4
- Hosea 3:4-5
- Joel 2:28-3:2, 9-21
- Amos 9:9-15
- Obadiah 1:15-21
- Micah 4:1-5:5
- Zephaniah 3:8-20
- Haggai 2:1-9
- Zechariah 2:1-13; 6:11-13; 8:1-8, 20-23; 9:9-10; 12:1-10; 14:1-21
- Malachi 3:1-5; 4:1-6
- Psalms 2:1-12; 22:1-21, 27-31; 24:1-10; 45:1-17; 46:1-11; 48:1-14; 67:1-7; 72:1-17; 89:1-50; 96:1-13; 98:1-9; 110:1-7

inauguration." That condition was given in the announcement by both John and Jesus when they said, "Repent!" Not only must Israel recognize Jesus as the King chosen by God (Deut 17:15), they must also meet the spiritual requirements for national repentance and personal holiness that were clearly stated in their Scriptures (e.g., Lev 11:45; 1 Kings 8:47; Ezek 18:29-32).

With this in mind, we see in Matt 5 - 7 that Jesus taught the principles of kingdom ethics in what is commonly called the Sermon on the Mount. In Matt 8 - 9 Jesus then authenticated His Messiahship by performing many miracles of healing, casting out demons, calming the wind and the waves during a storm on the Sea of Galilee, restoring a dead girl to life, and giving sight to the blind. It was at this time that Matthew started reporting direct opposition to Jesus from the Pharisees and religious rulers of Israel. In Matthew 10 Jesus commissioned His twelve disciples to travel throughout the nation, preaching the nearness of the kingdom, but only to the lost sheep of Israel.

Matthew 11 recorded that messengers from John the Baptist arrived with a question, and after answering them, Jesus gave an eloquent affirmation of John and his ministry. He also referred to His own rejection by the leaders of Israel (vv. 16-19), and He condemned the unrepentant cities of Israel in which He had ministered. One commentator said that, "the high ethical standards of the kingdom to come did not appeal to the Jewish people. In general, the Jewish people rejected Jesus, though many individuals became His followers. Because of this, Jesus turned to the individual rather than the nation as a whole, inviting each person to come to Him and find rest (Matt 11:28-30)." [Walvoord, 360]

This brings us up to "that day" which is mentioned in the first verse of Matthew 13. Some commentators have called this "The Busy Day" because so many events are recorded as taking place on that specific Sabbath day. In Matt 12:1-8 Jesus and His disciples were walking through a wheat field, where the disciples picked some heads of grain to eat. The Pharisees immediately accused Jesus of breaking the Sabbath, but Jesus skillfully defended their actions and ended by proclaiming Himself to be Lord of the Sabbath.

In Matt 12:9-14 Jesus taught in their synagogue, where the Pharisees set up a situation to accuse Him. After establishing that it was perfectly lawful to do good on the Sabbath, Jesus healed a man with a withered hand. But the Pharisees immediately began plotting how they would destroy Jesus. At this point, the nation's religious leaders had completely rejected

Him and His well-attested claims to be their Messiah and King.

In Matt 12:15-21 Jesus withdrew from the synagogue because He knew what they were planning, but many people followed Him and He healed those who were sick. His withdrawal from the developing conflict was in fulfillment of the prophecy in Isaiah 42:1-4 which confirmed Jesus as the One chosen by God. His fulfillment of this prophecy also hints at the coming time when the Gentile nations will put their hope in Him.

In Matt 12:22-32 a demon-possessed man is brought to Jesus, and we can imagine the Pharisees crowding around to see whether Jesus would again violate their Sabbath rules by healing him. Earlier that day Jesus had proven that it was lawful to do good on the Sabbath, so He immediately healed the man. The crowds were amazed, but the Pharisees accused Him of being in league with Satan. Jesus soundly refuted that charge, but it became clear that the religious leaders of Israel were guilty of the unforgivable sin against the Holy Spirit. There was no going back – the nation's leaders had completely rejected Jesus, and in Matt 12:33-37 Jesus condemned their hardened unbelief and depravity.

When the Pharisees attempted to get control of the situation by demanding a sign, as recorded in Matt 12:38-42, Jesus refused to give them anything further except the sign of Jonah. Not only did this prefigure the rejected King's death, burial, and resurrection, but Jesus declared that that generation of unbelieving Israelites would be condemned by Gentiles at the future judgment. The repentant people of both Nineveh and Sheba will rise up and condemn the unrepentant Israelites of that generation. The sign of Jonah also includes the concept of postponement. In the case of Nineveh, their repentance led God to postpone His judgment on Assyria for 150 years. In the case of the nation of Israel, their rejection of their King led to the postponement of His kingdom,

Jesus teaching in the synagogue and healing a demon-possessed man.

which is still yet to be realized.

In Matt 12:43-45 Jesus illustrated the condition of those Jews when He spoke of His purifying presence, warning them that unless Israel would fill the clean space with belief in their Messiah, their condition will end up worse than before. Around this time Jesus and His disciples entered a nearby house. In Matt 12:46-50 Jesus' mother and brothers arrived, but He aligned Himself with the family of faith rather than with earthly family ties.

We saw earlier in Matthew's account that the nearness of the kingdom had been proclaimed to the nation of Israel, first by John the Baptist (3:2), then by Jesus (4:17), and then by the twelve apostles (10:7). But from this point forward, the nearness of the kingdom is never mentioned again in the Gospels. Israel had rejected the King and His kingdom. The consequence of their rejection is that the prophesied kingdom would be postponed. As Jesus would later declare on His final journey to the Cross, "Jerusalem, Jerusalem, who kills the prophets and stones those who are sent to her! How often I wanted to gather your children together, the way a hen gathers her chicks under her wings, and you were unwilling. Behold, your house is being left to you desolate! For I say to you, from now on you will not see Me until you say, 'BLESSED IS HE WHO COMES IN THE NAME OF THE LORD!'" (Matt 23:37-39) Because of their rejection, the kingdom would not be instituted until a future time when the nation of Israel would recognize its Messiah and willingly meet the spiritual conditions for the establishment of the kingdom.

As we reflect on the first two words of Matt 13:1, we can see that the significant events which happened on "that day" are going to impact everything Jesus will say in the verses which follow. If we look at the end of this chapter we notice in verse 53 that all of this teaching took place on that same day. So, toward the end of that "Busy Day" Jesus left the house and walked to the seaside where He sat down.

**Matt 13:2 - And large crowds gathered to Him, so He got into a boat and sat down, and the whole crowd was standing on the beach.**

With so many people jostling to get close to Him, Jesus stepped into a boat, leaving the whole crowd standing along the shoreline. It is likely that some of Jesus' disciples were with Him in the boat, which was probably one of the larger fishing vessels belonging to Peter and Andrew or to James and John, the sons of Zebedee. Since Jesus sat down in the boat to teach, He likely would have needed help to keep the boat from drifting so that He could concentrate on addressing the people on the beach.

## Matt 13:3a - And He spoke many things to them in parables,

This is the first time in the Gospel of Matthew that we see the word **parable**. It is the Greek word *parabolē* which means "the placing of one thing beside another for the purpose of comparison to illustrate a spiritual or moral truth." One Jewish-Christian scholar has said,

> Perhaps no other mode of teaching was so common among the Jews as that of parables. Only in their case, they were almost entirely illustrations of what had been clearly said or taught; while, in the case of Christ, they served as the foundation for His teaching. [Edersheim in Constable]

So the way Jesus used parables was quite different from the traditional or typical way that the Jewish rabbis taught them. One Bible scholar observed that, "A parable is an utterance which does not carry its meaning on the surface, and which thus demands thought and perception if the hearer is to benefit from it. ... Far from giving explanations, parables themselves need to be explained." [France in Constable] This is an important fact to keep in mind as we study the parables of Jesus.

If we look through the Gospel of Matthew we see that earlier Jesus had shared several illustrations from nature and common life experience. These illustrations mainly occur in the Sermon on the Mount and they include the salt and the light (Matt 5:13-16), the birds and the lilies (Matt 6:26-30), the splinter and the beam in the eye (Matt 7:3-5), the two gates (Matt 7:13.), the wolves in sheep's clothing (Matt 7:15), the good and bad trees (Matt 7:17-19), and the wise and foolish builders (Matt 7:24-27). One commentator has said, "The

Sermon on the Mount discourse was not by any means lacking in illustration; still its main lines of thought were of the nature of direct spiritual instruction. But here there is no direct spiritual teaching. It is all indirect, it is parabolic through and through." [Expositor's in e-Sword] So, this tells us that there was a distinct change in the way Jesus began using parables to teach the multitudes.

In Matthew 13 Jesus will proceed to tell four parables to the mixed multitude, but He will not interpret the meaning of any of them for the crowd. Then privately Jesus will tell only His disciples the correct interpretation for two of the parables that He gave the multitude, and He will tell four additional parables only to His disciples. As was mentioned previously, in verse 53 we see that all of this teaching took place on that same day, so all of these parables should be viewed together as a unit. One Bible scholar provided a valuable insight into this group of parables:

> What Matthew thirteen provides is a cluster of eight parables with some (the first two) interpreted by Jesus and some stated without interpretation. Furthermore, the first and last parables serve as bookends to identify the general ideas of the entire cluster and to tie the cluster to the ongoing argument of the entire book of Matthew, taking into account the rejection of Jesus by the leaders of Israel and the subsequent development of something new in the transition from the focus on the Jews to the focus on Gentiles. The middle six parables flesh out more details with respect to these general themes. ... [Jesus] treats them all together seemingly as a unit. ... Consequently, one must study its connection to the others within the scheme of the whole. [Stallard, 328, 332]

This is the approach we will take in future chapters as we examine the parables in order to determine their message. In essence, Jesus' parables will reveal some of the important characteristics of the intervening time period between Israel's rejection of her King and their future acceptance of Him. These prophetic glimpses into the future are conveyed in pictures, and we will see how this new teaching method puzzled Jesus' disciples. In the next chapter we will look at Jesus' answer to the disciples' question about this change in teaching style, and He will explain why He began to use parables when talking to the people of Israel.

# The Reason for the Parables

## (Matthew 13:4-17)

In the last chapter we looked at the significance of the events which led up to Matthew 13. Israel's Messiah and King presented Himself to the nation and authenticated His claims in many ways. Even though Jesus offered the promised kingdom, there was intense opposition to Him from the leaders of Israel which culminated in their committing the unforgivable sin against the Holy Spirit. Their rejection of the King was final, and the kingdom could not and would not come until a future time when the nation meets the prerequisites for establishing that kingdom. One Bible commentator expressed it this way:

> This act of blasphemous unbelief on the part of the Jewish religious authorities was the turning point of Jesus' ministry. This was apparent in at least three important ways. First, from that time forward, He ceased to preach the message of the impending advent of the kingdom. The die was cast; because the Messiah had been rejected by those who must necessarily accept Him, the messianic kingdom would be delayed. Second, He began a transition in which he concentrated on His disciples rather than on the nation, preparing them for the ministry they would have following His ascension. And third, He began to teach in parables, which was an act of divine judgment upon Israel for their failure to receive the kingdom message. This third change is apparent immediately in Matthew's account, where the Lord Jesus not only teaches by means of these important Parables of the Kingdom, but also, in response to a private question from His disciples, explains the dual purpose for which He adopted this method of instruction (13:10–17). [Glass, 33-34]

As we mentioned in the last chapter, a parable does not display its meaning on the surface. Far from giving explanations, parables themselves need to be explained. So this is what the multitude would have been expecting as they waited on the beach, eagerly anticipating what Jesus would say as He sat in the boat to teach.

One thing we should recognize as we begin is the importance of the sequence or order of statements in Matthew 13. For example, we first see the Parable of the Sower which Jesus told the multitude. Because of the way He shared this story, the disciples were then prompted to ask Him why He was teaching the crowd that way. Jesus' answer to their question comes next, and it must come before His explanation of the parable, because His answer contained the key for understanding His interpretation of the parable. With this in mind, let's look at the Parable of the Sower.

**Matt 13:3-9 - And He spoke many things to them in parables, saying, "Behold, the sower went out to sow; and as he sowed, some seeds fell beside the road, and the birds came and ate them up. Others fell on the rocky places, where they did not have much soil; and immediately they sprang up, because they had no depth of soil. But when the sun had risen, they were scorched; and because they had no root, they withered away. Others fell among the thorns, and the thorns came up and choked them out. And others fell on the good soil and yielded a crop, some a hundredfold, some sixty, and some thirty. He who has ears, let him hear."**

This simple story was so true to life that Jesus might have been describing the actions of a farmer in a nearby field which He could see from the boat where He was teaching. When a person wanted to plant a large field of grain, he would walk through the plowed area with a bag of seed and fling handfuls of the seed away from himself in a broadcast pattern. This was a somewhat imprecise but highly effective method for planting a large field by hand. Depending on the skill of the sower, the majority of the seed would land in the plowed soil where it was intended to fall. Of course, a little bit of the seed would also land on the walking path, or in the shallow soil at the fringe of the field, or outside the field boundary where weeds and other natural plants were already growing. The sower only expected the seed that fell within the plowed ground to grow normally, and even those plants would yield varying results. That is basically what Jesus said to the crowds when He began teaching them from the boat.

We can imagine the people on the beach looking at each other with puzzled expressions, or maybe muttering to each other: "Is that all? Why is He telling us this? We already know how it works when you plant grain in a field." Even Jesus' disciples were wondering what was happening.

Jesus teaching from the boat with the multitudes on the shore.

**Matt 13:10 - And the disciples came and said to Him, "Why do You speak to them in parables?"**

When the text says "the disciples came" it uses the Greek word *proserchomai* which means "to draw near or come close." If they were with Him in the boat, we can imagine them leaning close to Him or even whispering their question to Him. In this chapter we are going to spend the bulk of our time studying Jesus' answer to this question.

**Matt 13:11 - Jesus answered them, "To you it has been granted to know the mysteries of the kingdom of heaven, but to them it has not been granted."**

The initial response of Jesus to their question has a simple structure: "To you it has been granted, but to them it has not been granted." The word **granted** is the Greek word *didōmi* which means "to give or furnish something to someone." Both words are in the perfect tense which indicates an action that occurred at some time in the past but which has results that continue into the present, and both words are in the passive voice which means that the subjects are the recipients of the action.

There are two things we should look at. First, who is doing the "granting." This verse uses "granted" in the same way as another of Jesus' statements which says, "For this reason I have said to you, that no one can come to Me unless it has been granted him from the Father" (John 6:65). In that case it was God the Father who was performing the action of granting or giving, and it is the same case in Matthew 13:11. It was a result of God's eternal counsels, decrees, and plans that certain people would be granted the privilege both of believing and of knowing the things of God.

As a side note here, the topic of the eternal counsels and plans of God is an interesting and important theological study, although it is not an easy subject. Ultimately it deals with the issues of divine sovereignty and human responsibility, but contemplating such deep truths is not for the faint of heart. As God told the prophet Isaiah, "'My thoughts are not your thoughts, Nor are your ways My ways,' declares the LORD. 'For as the heavens are higher than the earth, So are My ways higher than your ways and My thoughts than your thoughts.'" (Isaiah 55:8-9) Because of our finite human reasoning capabilities we may never fully comprehend this subject, but we can observe what God has revealed to us in His Word, and we can acknowledge it as true even though we may understand only a small part of it. The key truth in Matthew 13:11 is that God grants some things only to those He has chosen, which means there are others who are excluded.

The second thing we should look at in Matthew 13:11 is what is being granted. This is clearly stated in the passage: "To you it has been granted to know the mysteries of the kingdom of heaven." The phrase **to know** is the Greek word *ginōskō* which is a broad term for gaining knowledge. It can mean "to learn or to possess factual knowledge." So in this case there are some important truths that the disciples of Jesus are going to learn through His teaching in these parables. And the contrast here is that the unbelieving people who rejected Jesus as their King will not be able to know these truths.

The content of this new knowledge has to do with the "mysteries of the kingdom of heaven." The word **mystery** is the Greek word *mustērion* which is used in the New Testament to identify new revelation of knowledge that was hidden or unrevealed in the Old Testament. As it says in Deut 29:29, "The secret things belong to the Lord our God, but the things revealed belong to us and to our sons forever." God kept some of His plans secret until the proper time for them to be revealed. So a mystery refers to the secret thoughts, plans, and counsels of God which we cannot discover on our own, but which can only be known through divine revelation.

Here in Matthew 13:11 Jesus is saying that in these parables He is going to reveal some of the previously unrevealed parts of God's plan concerning the kingdom of heaven. In light of Israel's rejection of their King and the postponement of the kingdom, some previously unknown or unanticipated things will characterize the period of time between the Jews' rejection of Jesus and their acceptance of Him in the future. There are specific people to whom God has granted this new revelation, but there are others who are not given to understand.

This raises the question of what characterizes these two groups of people, so in the next verse Jesus continues by providing more explanation for what He has just said.

**Matt 13:12 - "For whoever has, to him more shall be given, and he will have an abundance; but whoever does not have, even what he has shall be taken away from him."**

In this verse Jesus begins by addressing those from the last verse to whom "it has been granted to know the mysteries of the kingdom." These are the ones identified here by the phrase "whoever has." The Greek word for **has** (*echō*) means "to have and to hold or possess; to keep something which has value."

We see in this verse that "to whoever has more will be given," and the word "given" is the same word that was translated "granted" in the previous verse. How much will they then have? The Greek word used here is *perisseuō* which means "to overflow with excess; to be in affluence." We might assume that to whoever has, more will be given in proportion to what he already has – but that is not what we see here. God's giving is not proportional. It is lavished upon them well beyond what they deserve and to such an extent that they could never imagine such an abundance.

In the next part of this verse, these favored people are contrasted with "whoever does not have," and we might assume that Jesus would say, "To whoever does not have, more will not be given." That would correspond to the logic in the previous verse: there it was "granted vs. not granted" ... so it would make sense that here it should be "given vs. not given." But Jesus goes well beyond this when He says that not only will no more be given to those people, but even what they have will be taken away. Even what they "hold onto as being valuable" will be shown to be of no value at all.

One Bible commentator described the situation of those to whom Jesus ministered when he said:

All these men among whom the ministry of Jesus had been exercised had preliminary knowledge of the ways of God as a result of the [Jewish] religion in which they had been born and trained. In fulfillment of the messages of their own Scriptures He had come. Certain of them had received Him, others of them had rejected Him. To those receiving Him were given the mysteries of the Kingdom. To those rejecting Him these messages could not be given, and they were in danger of losing the real value of all that they had gained through their early religious training. ... What was the essential difference between the disciples and the rulers and multitudes standing around? Did it not lie here, that the disciples had received Jesus as King, and by reason of that action and their attitude towards Him had become able to receive the mysteries of His Kingdom? The people had rejected Him up to this time, and therefore He could not give to them, nor could they have received, the mysteries of the Kingdom. To the men who had crowned Him, He belonged; and all the principles and privileges of the Kingdom they were able to appreciate and possess. The others had so far refused their allegiance and were therefore unable to see, or enter into the Kingdom. [Morgan, 21, 22]

I think this is an important comment which points us back to the context for these parables of Jesus. The majority of the people who should have repented and accepted their King had rejected Him instead. They did not have Him in the sense of possessing something of value. Early in the teaching ministry of Jesus He had said, "For I say to you that unless your righteousness surpasses that of the scribes and Pharisees, you will not enter the kingdom of heaven" (Matt 5:20). But how does a person obtain righteousness? It certainly does not come by obeying a strict set of external rules and regulations, which was what the scribes and Pharisees were doing and teaching.

These people should have known from their Scriptures that God's righteousness can only be obtained through faith. They considered themselves to be children of Abraham, the first Hebrew and the father of their nation. He was the primary example of someone who was righteous before God. But Abraham did not obtain righteousness by following a strict set of rules and regulations. Genesis 15:6 says that Abraham "believed in the LORD; and He reckoned it to him as righteousness." Throughout the Old Testament we see others who followed the example of Abraham in obtaining righteousness only by believing God. Righteousness can only be obtained by having it reckoned or credited to your account by God. There is nothing that a sinful human being can do to earn it. It is granted only through trusting in God.

When Jesus gave the Sermon on the Mount and said, "unless your righteousness surpasses that of the scribes and Pharisees, you will not enter the kingdom of heaven" (Matt 5:20), there were many individuals who believed in Him and accepted Him as their Messiah. Because they desired to have (*echō*) and to hold onto Jesus as being of great value – believing Him to be God's chosen Messiah – their faith was reckoned to them as righteousness. Because of their faith and trust in Him, righteousness was credited to their account. One commentator expressed it this way: "God requires kingdom righteousness of the subjects of His kingdom, but such righteousness can be experienced only in that person who permits the King to reign in his life." [Strauss, 28] Their ac-

| Whoever has (Haves) | Whoever does not have (Have Nots) |
|---|---|
| Recognized Jesus as God's chosen King | Rejected Jesus as God's chosen King |
| Repented when the kingdom was proclaimed | No repentance when the kingdom proclaimed |
| Believed and trusted in Jesus as Messiah | Did not believe in Jesus as their Messiah |
| God granted new revelation of His plan | God did not grant understanding of His plan |

ceptance of God's chosen Messiah opened the way for them to participate in the coming kingdom of heaven, and it also granted them more knowledge of the mysteries, which consisted of new revelation of God's plan for the kingdom of heaven. This is what Jesus means when He says, "whoever has, to him more shall be given, and he will have an abundance; but whoever does not have, even what he has shall be taken away from him."

The chart at the top of this page shows some of the differences between these two groups of people.

**Matt 13:13 - "Therefore I speak to them in parables; because while seeing they do not see, and while hearing they do not hear, nor do they understand."**

This verse begins with the word **therefore** which connects it to what has just been said. It is because of the characteristics particularly of the "have nots" that Jesus will use parables to teach them. The majority of the Jewish people to whom Jesus ministered exhibited the same traits as their forefathers to whom the Old Testament prophets ministered. For example, Jeremiah said to the Jews of his day, "Now hear this, O foolish and senseless people, Who have eyes but do not see; Who have ears but do not hear" (Jer 5:21). And God told Ezekiel, "You live in the midst of the rebellious house, who have eyes to see but do not see, ears to hear but do not hear; for they are a rebellious house" (Ezek 12:2). The Israelites were no different in Jesus' day than they had been in the days of the prophets.

One commentator described their condition by saying, "Christ declares in effect that these people did not see the things that His disciples saw. They saw without seeing, they heard without hearing. And why? They had shut their eyes lest they should see, and they had stopped their ears lest they should hear. They had rejected the King at the commencement of His ministry, and without the King they had no key to the mysteries of the Kingdom." [Morgan, 23-24]

In a way, the fact that Jesus began teaching in parables came from His desire to show mercy to those who refused to see and hear. The biblical principle is that greater knowledge always results in greater accountability. As one commentator has said, "Jesus ... presented God's message so the spiritually sensitive could understand, but the hardened would merely hear a story without heaping up additional condemnation for rejecting God's Word." [Guzik in e-Sword]

At the end of this verse Jesus says, "nor do they understand." **Understand** is the Greek word *suniēmi* which means "to put together mentally or to comprehend." It involves assembling the facts into an organized whole, like collecting all of the pieces of a jigsaw puzzle and putting them together. In the New Testament it is often found in the quotations of Old Testament texts, and that seems to be the sense which is intended here in Matthew 13. One lexicon has said about this word, "On the one hand, to understand is a gift from God, but on the other hand, the inability to understand or the lack of insight is a result of one's own disobedience and unfaithfulness." [Mounce, 758]

So, here in Matthew 13, the Israelites' lack of understanding is the result of their own hardness of heart and the rejection of their King. Jesus will now cite Old Testament support for this conclusion in the next two verses.

**Matt 13:14 - "In their case the prophecy of Isaiah is being fulfilled, which says, 'YOU WILL KEEP ON HEARING, BUT WILL NOT UNDERSTAND; YOU WILL KEEP ON SEEING, BUT WILL NOT PERCEIVE;'"**

This verse introduces Jesus' quote from Isaiah 6:9-10. This passage originally appeared in the context of God's calling of Isaiah to his ministry as a prophet. From the very beginning Isaiah was told that he would preach to a nation whose people would not receive his message but would instead reject it. Yet Isaiah dutifully proclaimed God's Word, knowing in advance that the people would not listen. This is a striking parallel to the situation Jesus faced as described in the Gospel of Matthew. The prophecy of Isaiah 6 was literally fulfilled by the people in Isaiah's day, but in Jesus' day the Israelites exhibited exactly the same character. Like their forefathers, they closed their eyes to the truth and rejected God's message. As one commentator has said, "The words of Isaiah were therefore as well fitted to express the character of the people in the time of Christ as in that of the prophet. In this sense they were fulfilled or filled up; that is, a case occurred that corresponded to their meaning." [Barnes in e-Sword] In other words, this prophecy provided the perfect biblical precedent for Jesus' response to people who exhibited these characteristics.

Jesus spoke in a way that the hardened multitudes could hear but not understand, and see but not perceive. This passage could be translated literally as, "hearing you will hear, and you will not understand" followed by "seeing you will see, and you will not perceive." Receiving important information

23

through the five senses should trigger thought processes that result in personal understanding and insight, but in their case it did not. One commentator explained it this way:

> A parable has the great virtue that it enables and compels a man to discover truth for himself. It does not do a man's thinking for him. It says, "Here is a story. What is the truth in it? Think it out for yourself." ... The other side of that is that the parable conceals truth from those who are either too lazy to think or too blinded by prejudice to see. It puts the responsibility fairly and squarely on the individual. It reveals truth to him who desires truth; it conceals truth from him who does not wish to see the truth. [Barclay, 55, 56]

So in the case of the "have nots" whom Jesus was speaking about, their receptivity ended when the story was finished.

**Matt 13:15 - "FOR THE HEART OF THIS PEOPLE HAS BECOME DULL, WITH THEIR EARS THEY SCARCELY HEAR, AND THEY HAVE CLOSED THEIR EYES, OTHERWISE THEY WOULD SEE WITH THEIR EYES, HEAR WITH THEIR EARS, AND UNDERSTAND WITH THEIR HEART AND RETURN, AND I WOULD HEAL THEM."**

In this verse the quote from Isaiah goes on to describe the condition of "the heart of this people," which has "become dull." The Greek word translated **dull** is *pachunō* which means "to thicken or become calloused to the point of insensitivity." Next we see that their ears **scarcely hear** which uses the Greek word *bareōs* meaning "heavily or with difficulty." Finally we see the state of their eyes, which "they have closed." The Hebrew verb (*hasha*) in the original passage can mean "to smear over" with wax or some other substance so that the eyes cannot be opened. [See Clarke comment on Isa 6:10 in e-Sword.]

The first part of this verse accurately described the condition of the Israelites' ears and eyes. But the last part of the verse describes what might happen if this sad situation were not true. Working backward from seeing with their eyes, to hearing with their ears, and understanding with their heart – if they were to truly understand then they would return and God would heal them. The Greek word translated as **return** is *epistrephō* which can mean "to turn around, to turn back, to return, or even to be converted." To **heal** can mean to heal physically or to restore spiritually from a state of sin. Unfortunately for the Israelites the first part of the verse was true of them, rather than the last part. One commentator has said:

> Their ignorance was willful ignorance. They did not understand because they would not understand. Theirs was a deliberate rejection of the truth. ... They did it themselves, deliberately, voluntarily, and knowingly. They knew what God's plan was for them, but they did not want it, choosing rather their own folly and fleshly desires. Isaiah said the people would close their own eyes lest they should see, and turn a deaf ear on the truth lest they should hear. And that is why Jesus said, 'Who hath ears to hear, let him hear'. Any person who anesthetizes his heart, muffles his ears, and shuts his eyes to the Word of God, God will punish by allowing him to have his way. [Strauss, 34, 35]

Now, from these last three verses we need to remember several concepts that will provide the key for interpreting the Parable of the Sower:

- Seeing and hearing did not lead to understanding and perceiving
- The condition of the heart was insensitive
- The people were accountable for closing their eyes and ears
- They failed to turn to the Lord, whether for salvation or understanding

Jesus now moves on to discuss the condition of His faithful followers, which is quite different.

**Matt 13:16 - "But blessed are your eyes, because they see; and your ears, because they hear."**

But, by contrast, Jesus then described the status of His faithful followers. They are the "haves" who have put their trust in Jesus as their Messiah. They are truly blessed because they can understand what He is teaching them. The Greek word for **blessed** is *makarios*, which is the same word recorded in the Beatitudes from the Sermon on the Mount. It is the same word with the same meaning as when Jesus said, "Blessed are those who hunger and thirst for righteousness, for they shall be satisfied" (Matt 5:6).

In contrast to those who had hardened their hearts, muffled their ears, and closed their eyes, everyone who eagerly opened their eyes to see and their ears to hear and their hearts to understand will receive immense blessings.

**Matt 13:17 - "For truly I say to you that many prophets and righteous men desired to see what you see, and did not see it, and to hear what you hear, and did not hear it."**

Here Jesus provides additional explanation for what He just said about the blessings given to His faithful followers. He clearly pictures the privileged status of His disciples, compared to all of the righteous ones who had gone before them. The many prophets and righteous men who had been used by God to accomplish such amazing things throughout the Old Testament would have given anything to be in the disciples place – to actually be in the presence of their Messiah, the One whose coming had been predicted from Genesis 3:15 up to the last verse of Malachi's prophecy.

Matthew 13:17 says that they desired to see what Jesus' followers saw, and the Greek word translated **desired** is *epithumeō*. This is an intensified form of the word for passion. It is not a simple desire but a passionate longing for something, which is sometimes translated "to covet." As one commentator expressed it, "Not only were the disciples blessed above the blinded just spoken of, but favored above the most honored and the best that ever lived under the old economy, who had but glimpses of these things, just sufficient to kindle in them desires not to be fulfilled to any in their day." [JFB in e-Sword] So those righteous ones of past ages looked forward in hope to the time when the events would occur that Jesus' disciples were privileged to experience in person.

What Jesus said here was later expressed by the writer of the Book of Hebrews when he said, "All these died in faith, without receiving the promises, but having seen them and having welcomed them from a distance, and having confessed that they were strangers and exiles on the earth" (Heb 11:13). The apostle Peter also wrote about this when he said, "The prophets who prophesied of the grace that would come to you made careful searches and inquiries, seeking to know what person or time the Spirit of Christ within them was indicating as He predicted the sufferings of Christ and the glories to follow. It was revealed to them that they were not serving themselves, but you, in these things which now have been announced to you through those who preached the gospel to you by the Holy Spirit sent from heaven—things into which angels long to look" (1 Peter 1:10-12).

The prophets of the Old Testament were shown many important things. They had clues about the sufferings of the Messiah, and of course they were given a wealth of information about the glorious kingdom that would be established by Messiah on earth where He would sit on David's throne in Jerusalem to rule over the nations. But there were still some secrets of God's plan for the ages which remained unrevealed to the Old Testament prophets. These are the mysteries which Jesus and the later writers of the New Testament would reveal. One commentator explained it this way:

> The prophets saw the coming golden age, but they did not see the time period between Christ's two appearings, now more than nineteen hundred years. They saw both His sufferings and the glory that would follow (1 Peter 1:10-11), but the time between

those two events was the mystery about which they searched diligently. The kingdom of heaven was no secret to Israel. The mystery was the fact that there would be a long period of time, including the church age, in which God would not deal with Israel as a nation but would send the gospel into all the world. God, in His compassion for the entire race of mankind, purposed from eternity to redeem people from every tribe and nation. This is the great mystery, that God would set aside His chosen people Israel, so that He might redeem sinners from among the Gentiles as well as Jews. [Strauss, 39]

So as we consider these two verses, where Jesus explained how blessed His followers were compared to the righteous ones of past ages, we should think about how much more blessed we are in our time because we have even more revelation than Jesus' disciples did at that time. When Jesus told His disciples, "Blessed are your eyes, because they see; and your ears, because they hear," think about what Jesus would say to us, considering all of the benefits and privileges we have been given. And we need to remember that "from everyone who has been given much, much will be required; and to whom they entrusted much, of him they will ask all the more" (Luke 12:48).

# Interpreting the Parable
## of the Sower

### (Matthew 13:18-23)

In this chapter we'll look at the explanation which Jesus gave only to His disciples for the Parable of the Sower. As we begin, let's refresh our memory about this parable. As He was sitting in the boat Jesus spoke these words to the multitude who were standing on the beach.

**Matt 13:3-9 - And He spoke many things to them in parables, saying, "Behold, the sower went out to sow; and as he sowed, some seeds fell beside the road, and the birds came and ate them up. Others fell on the rocky places, where they did not have much soil; and immediately they sprang up, because they had no depth of soil. But when the sun had risen, they were scorched; and because they had no root, they withered away. Others fell among the thorns, and the thorns came up and choked them out. And others fell on the good soil and yielded a crop, some a hundredfold, some sixty, and some thirty. He who has ears, let him hear."**

Immediately His disciples asked why Jesus was teaching the crowd this way, and He answered by describing the spiritual condition of the multitude in Israel. He told them privately that there were two kinds of people, which we called the "haves" and the "have nots" in the last chapter. In order to become one of the "haves," a person must hear the word of the kingdom: "Repent, for the kingdom of heaven is at hand!" and he must respond to the word of the kingdom with understanding and repentance, believing in Jesus as the Messiah and King. Those people met the spiritual qualifications for participating in the kingdom of heaven. In the next parable Jesus will call them "sons" or heirs of the kingdom.

Unfortunately, the majority of the nation of Israel did not respond with understanding and repentance. In the last chapter we called this second group the "have nots" and Jesus described them as being like their forefathers, whose hearts had become insensitive, whose ears barely hear, and who had deliberately closed their eyes and refused to perceive. Christ's description of the multitude in His day contains the key to His explanation of the Parable of the Sower.

The word of the kingdom had been proclaimed to them, so they heard the message which included truths about the spiritual qualifications for establishing the kingdom. It required both understanding and accepting Jesus as the Messiah as well as personally turning to God in repentance. At the end of Jesus' quote from Isaiah 6:9-10 it says, "For the heart of this people has become dull, with their ears they scarcely hear, and they have closed their eyes, otherwise they would see with their eyes, hear with their ears, and understand with their heart and return, and I would heal them." This is why Jesus spoke to the crowd in parables. As He said in verse 13, "because while seeing they do not see, and while hearing they do not hear, nor do they understand" (Matt 13:13).

Essentially, Jesus told the Parable of the Sower to illustrate several of the reasons why the multitude in Israel were not responding to the word of the kingdom. This parable, along with the disciples' question, Jesus' answer, and His interpretation, serve as a transition into the group of six "kingdom parables" which will include "the mysteries of the kingdom of heaven" that Jesus promised in Matt 13:11. As one Bible scholar has said,

The word of the kingdom had been proclaimed to Israel by John, by Jesus, and by the disciples. This parable notes the blindness and dullness of Israel's response to this proclamation. However, some did understand and were growing in understanding. ... The word of the kingdom received into the heart would yield more revelation and understanding of it. This new revelation is that which the King is about to give in the remainder of Matthew 13. [Toussaint-B, 179]

So we could say that the Parable of the Sower is a parable about why Jesus began teaching in parables. With this in mind, let's begin looking at Jesus' private explanation to the disciples for the meaning of this parable.

## Matt 13:18 - "Hear then the parable of the sower."

Literally, this could be translated: "You, therefore, hear." The plural **you** is put first in this sentence for emphasis. This focuses His message directly on the small group of faithful

Behold, the Sower
went out to sow.

followers that He expects will hear and understand. The word **then** could also be translated "therefore" and it connects this verse to what Jesus had just said when He declared, "Blessed are your eyes, because they see; and your ears, because they hear" (Matt 13:16). The disciples were part of the small group who "have" and to whom more shall be given (Matt 13:12).

It was because of the disciples' favored status as members of the "haves" – ones who heard and understood the word of the kingdom, and who turned to God in faith and repentance – that God granted them the knowledge of the mysteries of the kingdom of heaven which Jesus will reveal in the upcoming parables. But before sharing those truths, He wants the disciples to see why He spoke to the crowd in parables. And that is what the Parable of the Sower is all about.

Notice that when Jesus spoke this parable He did not say "The kingdom of heaven is like..." This first parable as well as the final parable in this chapter are unique in that they do not have this phrase identifying the topic or subject of the parable. As one commentator expressed it,

> The parable of the Seed and the Sower is the only one of the [first] seven parables that does not begin with the formula, "The kingdom of heaven is like..." and is therefore both transitional and introductory to the other parables, not itself providing any new truth regarding the kingdom of heaven. [Glass, 115]

So this parable is intended to give several examples of issues that can lead to the conditions described in the prophecy of Isaiah 6:9-10 where it says, "the heart of this people has become dull, with their ears they scarcely hear, and they have closed their eyes," ultimately resulting in their failure to understand with their heart and turn to the Lord. Let's now look at Jesus' explanation for the first part of this parable.

**Matt 13:19 - "When anyone hears the word of the kingdom and does not understand it, the evil one comes and snatches away what has been sown in his heart. This is the one on whom seed was sown beside the road."**

The first phrase literally says, "Anyone hearing the word of the kingdom and not understanding." **Understanding** is a form of the same Greek word (*suniēmi*) which is translated "understand" three times in Jesus' previous response to the disciples' question. The first thing we should do is examine the description Jesus gave in answer to their question to see if we can determine who this person is. As Jesus had said in Matt 13:13, "while hearing they do not hear, nor do they understand." So this first person being described in the Parable of the Sower is a member of the "have nots" whose heart had become insensitive, whose ears barely hear, and who had deliberately closed their eyes and refused to understand.

As we saw previously, the "word of the kingdom" is the message that was proclaimed by John the Baptist, by Jesus, and by the disciples: "Repent, for the kingdom of heaven is at hand!" This message included the requirement both for repentance and turning to the Lord, accepting and believing in Jesus as the Messiah and King. In the case of this first person in the Parable of the Sower, however, Jesus had said, "Some seeds fell beside the road, and the birds came and ate them up" (Matt 13:4). Here in His explanation it literally says, "The evil one comes and snatches that which had been sown in his heart."

We see here that the word of the kingdom had been proclaimed to this person, and (although he could barely hear) the text says that he did hear the message. But (according to Jesus' answer to His disciples) this man's heart was insensitive, calloused, or hardened, like the thick, dry husk of a seed.

This person's heart was closed to the word of the kingdom so that message was easily snatched away by his adversary the devil. Here verse 19 presents the "worst case scenario" of a hardened Israelite who refused to understand the word of the kingdom or allow it to impact his life. The scribes and Pharisees who bitterly opposed Jesus are biblical examples of this type of person.

In the last phrase of this verse, Jesus identified this person as "the one on whom seed was sown beside the road." That wording from the NAS95 version is somewhat awkward, and it isn't any clearer in the NKJV which says, "This is he who received seed by the wayside." The original American Standard Version captures the Greek phrase more literally when it says, "This is he that was sown by the wayside." The surprising thing that becomes evident in this verse is that the Greek pronouns and participles are all in the masculine gender. One Greek language scholar has said, "Matthew, like Mark, speaks of the people who hear the words as the seed itself." [Robertson in e-Sword] And another Bible commentator expressed it this way: "The use of the masculine demonstrative pronoun in verses 19, 22, and 23, as well as the masculine participle, has caused some difficulty. The pronoun and the participle cannot refer to the seed since the word seed is neuter in gender." [Toussaint-B, 180] Several features stand out as we look at a flow diagram of a literal translation of Matt 13:19 (top of page 35).

All of the words highlighted in gray are in the masculine gender, and the participles and verbs are in the present tense. The only participle not in the masculine gender is the one identifying what had been previously sown, which matches the neuter gender for seed. That participle is also the only one in the perfect tense, which indicates an action that occurred in the past with consequences that continued into the present. This could represent the initial proclamation of the word of the kingdom. Whatever interpretation we give to this

## Matthew 13:19

Anyone

> pres act participle
> **hearing** and
> pres act participle
> <u>not</u> **understanding** ⎬ the word
> └─ of the kingdom

the evil one ⎨ pres act verb
**comes** and
pres act verb
**snatches** ⎬ perfect passive participle (dir obj)
that previously sown
└─ in the heart of him

subject     pres act participle
This one **is**   he being sown
└─ along the road

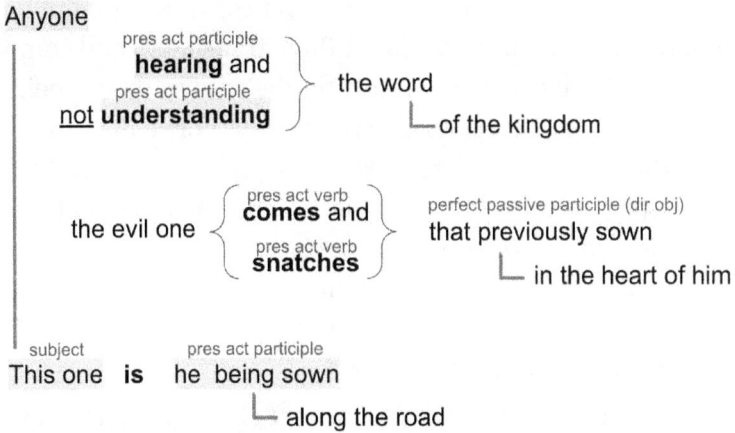

verse, it must remain true to the actual text of this passage that we see here.

Most of the early Bible expositors translated this phrase literally. One Greek language scholar went so far as to say that it would be inaccurate to translate it as, "This is he in whose case the seed was sown upon the road." And this is similar to how many of today's Bible versions translate this passage. This particular scholar explained why such a paraphrase is inaccurate:

> One might perhaps acquiesce in such inaccuracy of expression as this paraphrase supposes, if the identification of the seed with the persons occurred only in this one passage. But a glance at the sequel shows that this identification recurs in the interpretation of each one of the four parts of the parable. If we add, further, the preliminary observation, that in the parable immediately following, which treats in like manner the sowing of seed and its growth, the seed is from the first expressly interpreted of persons and persons only, it remains without doubt that the present passage can only be explained in the light of this general phenomenon. [Goebel, 46-47]

When people read the original story told by Jesus, what they see is the different types of soil being mentioned. But the differences in the soil do not rule out the possibility that there are also differences in the seed, differences which are implicit but not overtly mentioned. Most Bible translators and commentators have decided to interpret the seed as the gospel, with the different responses to the gospel represented by the soils. They interpret the seed as a uniformly consistent thing (the gospel), with the diverse soils accounting for all of the differences in response. On the surface this seems to be a reasonable interpretation of the original story. But when we examine Jesus' own explanation of the story, something unexpected appears.

The seed does not have a consistent character; it is not of uniform quality. As any farmer might tell us, the quality of seed itself can vary widely even within the same batch. Several seeds can fall right next to each other in a plowed field and one will grow normally while the other will never germinate. On the other hand, even if several seeds fall on hard-packed ground or among the weeds, sometimes a few of them will grow normally even under such adverse conditions. The point here is that the seed itself can be of widely different character, which can account for the different responses.

I'd like to share an extended quote from a commentator of a previous century who expressed the interpretation of this verse in a way that we may not typically hear today. He said this:

> Listening to the parable we should certainly be inclined to think that the chief lessons were to be learnt from the nature of the soil. ... When however we turn to Christ's explanation, we find that such is not the case, but rather that the chief lessons of the parable are those concerning the nature of the seed. Without His explanation we should inevitably say that the harvest depends upon whether the nature of the soil be the open highway, or the rocky places of the fields, or the thorny ground, or the fruitful ground. Jesus, however, lays no emphasis upon the soil, but all

emphasis upon the condition of the seed which is cast into the soil. This is a most important distinction to be kept carefully in mind, or we shall continue to misinterpret the parable. I am aware that this statement may seem at first to obscure the vision of truth, contradicting, as it does, popular conceptions of the teaching of this parable.

Notice most carefully here the actual words: "This is he that was sown by the wayside." Not, this is it, but this is he. "And he that was sown upon the rocky places, this is he that heareth the word, and straightway with joy receiveth it." Again notice the words, he that was sown; not it, but he. "And he that was sown among the thorns, this is he that heareth the word." Once more, he that was sown, not it. "And he that was sown upon the good ground, this is he that heareth the word." Thus finally, he that was sown, not it. We have generally regarded the '"sower" of this parable as a type first of our Lord Himself, and then of all those who preach the word, and the seed as the word sown in the hearts of men who respond to it in different ways according to their nature. This is a treatment of the parable which contradicts absolutely Christ's own explanation of it. In that explanation He declares, not that the sowing of the seed is the word cast into the heart of a man, but that it is the casting of a man into a certain situation. The sowing here referred to, then, to state the case broadly, is the sowing, not of truth, but of men, for in the next parable, where the Lord again takes up the figure of sowing, He distinctly says of the good seed, "These are the sons of the Kingdom." This truth is emphasized too in the first parable by the fact that, in every instance in His explanation, the King said, "he that was sown." [Morgan, 53-56]

I think this comment is one which we should carefully consider as we seek to accurately interpret this passage of Scripture. Knowing that the seed itself is what accounts for the difference in responsiveness could assist those who are trying to accurately translate this passage – and it would hopefully eliminate some of the awkward wording that we see in different Bible versions today. Whenever possible we should simply say what the original text says. Given our own interpretation of a parable versus Jesus' interpretation of that same parable, the interpretation of Jesus is always definitive.

So, what practical difference does it make to the point of the parable if the different responses of people are represented as soils or seeds? In either case the message is clear: a hard-hearted person who refuses to understand and respond to the word of the kingdom will be an easy target for the devil to remove all possibility of understanding. If that occurs, this person will suffer the consequences for his rejection of the truth. It is important, however, for us to remain true to the original text of Scripture as we seek to accurately translate and interpret these passages.

With this in mind, let's look now at Jesus' second illustration for how the word of the kingdom can be rendered ineffective.

**Matt 13:20-21 - "The one on whom seed was sown on the rocky places, this is the man who hears the word and immediately receives it with joy; yet he has no firm root in himself, but is only temporary, and when affliction or persecution arises because of the word, immediately he falls away."**

As was mentioned previously, Jesus told the Parable of the Sower to illustrate several of the reasons why the multitude in Israel were not responding to the word of the kingdom. Here in these two verses we see a second example. In the case of this second person, Jesus' parable had said, "Immediately they sprang up, because they had no depth of soil" (Matt 13:5). One commentator explained this type of germination by saying,

> The stony ground was not ground filled with stones; it was what was common in Palestine, a thin skin of earth on top of an underlying shelf of limestone rock. The earth might be only a few inches deep before the rock was reached. On such ground the seed would certainly germinate; and it would germinate quickly, because the ground grew speedily warm with the heat of the sun. But there was no depth of earth and when it sent down its roots in search of nourishment and moisture, it would meet only the

rock, and would be starved to death, and quite unable to withstand the heat of the sun. [Barclay, 58]

Here in Jesus' explanation of this verse, however, there is again a somewhat awkward translation of the Greek text. This could be translated literally, "And this one is he being sown on the rocky places; this is he who is hearing the word, and immediately with joy is receiving it." We see again that the word of the kingdom had been proclaimed to this person, and the text says that he heard the message and actually received it with joy. The Greek word for **received** is *lambano* which is a broad term that means "to take something that is given." The response is described as an emotional response, rather than a soul-searching, life-changing understanding and repentance. One commentator has said,

Many hearts are thin and shallow. They respond readily to any new thing. They follow new fashions, respond enthusiastically to a famous personality who is popular at the time. They are the emotional type who are swept off their feet easily. They hear the Word and with lighthearted joy respond to it, but they are shallow and have no depth. These stony-ground hearers heard the Word and showed an outward enthusiasm for it for a while. [Strauss, 46]

Even though the initial response seemed positive, Jesus explained that it didn't require much external pressure to neutralize the word of the kingdom. He said, "Yet he has no firm root in himself, but is only temporary, and when affliction or persecution arises because of the word, immediately he falls away."

As Jesus explained it, the problem is that this person had no root in himself. The word **root** is the Greek word *rhiza* from which we get our English word rhizome. It would make more sense to say this person "had no root in himself" if we were figuratively representing a man as a seed, rather than as the soil. Soil does not generate roots, but seeds do generate roots from within themselves. So Jesus is speaking of a man that is either incapable or unwilling to put out roots which will allow him to anchor himself in the truth and take in nourishment so he can grow.

Jesus' description means that the word of the kingdom, with its requirement for personal repentance and trust in the Messiah, never impacted the person's heart to the point where he began to put out roots. Even though this person may have seemed receptive initially, he was unwilling to make a deep, lasting commitment to the truth of the word. External pressures quickly neutralized it. The word **affliction** is the Greek word *thlipsis* which means "pressure or oppression." And the word **persecution** is the Greek word *diōgmos* which means "intimidation or harassment, especially for religious reasons."

The New Testament shares several instances of this kind of response. For example, after Jesus healed a man who was born blind, the Pharisees questioned the man's parents, but they chose to plead ignorance about the situation, "because they were afraid of the Jews; for the Jews had already agreed that if anyone confessed Him to be Christ, he was to be put out of the synagogue" (John 9:22). In another case several of the religious leaders initially believed in Jesus, "but because of the Pharisees they were not confessing Him, for fear that they would be put out of the synagogue; for they loved the approval of men rather than the approval of God" (John 12:42-43).

So, here in this verse Jesus provided a second illustration for why the multitude in Israel were not responding to the word of the kingdom due to external pressures.

**Matt 13:22 - "And the one on whom seed was sown among the thorns, this is the man who hears the word, and the worry of the world and the deceitfulness of wealth choke the word, and it becomes unfruitful."**

In this verse we see a third way that the word of the kingdom was rendered ineffective. In the case of this third person, Jesus' parable had said, "Others fell among the thorns, and the thorns came up and choked them out" (Matt 13:7).

Here in His explanation of this verse, there is again a somewhat awkward translation of the Greek text. Literally this could be translated, "And he being sown among the thorns, this is he who is hearing the word." We see that the word of the kingdom had been proclaimed to this person, and the text says that he heard the message. Jesus explained that in this case it didn't require much internal pressure to make the word of the kingdom ineffective. He said, "The worry of the world and the deceitfulness of wealth choke the word, and it becomes unfruitful."

**Worry** is the Greek word *merimna* which comes from a root word that means "divided or distracted." When we see a phrase like "worry of the world" we often assume that **world** is translated from the Greek word *kosmos*, meaning the world system around us. But that is not the word used here. This verse uses the Greek word *aiōn* which is often translated as "age" meaning the period of time in which we are living. Every age has different distractions and worries, so this verse would apply universally to people living at any period of time throughout history.

**Deceitfulness** is the Greek word *apatē* which comes from a root word meaning "to cheat or to seduce into error." And to **choke** is the word *sumpnigō* which means "to press around or crowd a person so as to suffocate him." As in the case of external pressure, here the internal pressures of distraction and materialism suffocate the word of the kingdom. Its requirement for personal repentance and trust in the Messiah never affect this person to the point of changing his priorities in life. One commentator described it this way:

Such a person permits life's competing subjects of concern to take precedence over the priority of his or her spiritual development (cf. 19:16-22). The present life, rather than the life to come, and present treasure, rather than future treasure, capture this person's affections. These things are deceitful because they can drain spiritual vitality before the person realizes what is happening to him or her. Interestingly, the enemy of fruitfulness in the first instance is the devil, in the second instance it is the world, and in the third instance it is the flesh (1 John 2:15-17). [Constable]

The New Testament also describes several instances of this kind of behavior. For example, a man who said he had kept the Law's commandments from his youth, asked Jesus, "What shall I do to inherit eternal life?" Mark 10:21-22 says, "Looking at him, Jesus felt a love for him and said to him, 'One thing you lack: go and sell all you possess and give to the poor, and you will have treasure in heaven; and come, follow Me.' But at these words he was saddened, and he went away grieving, for he was one who owned much property."

So, here in Matt 13:21-22 Jesus gave a third illustration for why the multitude in Israel did not respond to the word of the kingdom because of their own self-centered values and priorities.

**Matt 13:23 - "And the one on whom seed was sown on the good soil, this is the man who hears the word and understands it; who indeed bears fruit and brings forth, some a hundredfold, some sixty, and some thirty."**

Finally, Jesus finished the Parable of the Sower by explaining the seed which grew in the good soil. His parable had said that it "yielded a crop, some a hundredfold, some sixty, and some thirty" (Matt 13:8). And here in verse 23 He explained the difference in this seed. Literally it could be translated, "And the one being sown on the good ground: this is he who is hearing and is understanding the word." It is clear that

Jesus is addressing the one "to whom more shall be given, so that he will have an abundance" (Matt 13:12). The difference is that his heart is responsive and he understands the word of the kingdom, which results in believing in Jesus as the Messiah and turning to God in repentance. One commentator has said:

> This is the person who understands the message about the messianic kingdom when he or she hears it, and responds appropriately to it. This would involve believing in Jesus. Such a person eventually becomes spiritually productive, though the degree of productivity varies. However, Jesus commended all who received the message of the messianic kingdom and believed it, regardless of their measure of productivity. [Constable]

In this verse Jesus explained that the result is due to differences in the quality of the seed rather than solely on differences in soil conditions. All of the seed in this verse falls side by side into the same good plowed soil, but the results vary based on the character of the seed itself: some produce a hundredfold, some sixty, and some thirty. As Dr. Morgan has said,

> If [this parable] is interpreted in the usual way, then there is no responsibility whatever upon the seed, neither can the soil be blamed for the lack of result due to its own natural hardness, for it cannot help being what it is. But when we come to our Lord's explanation we find how serious our responsibility is, for He teaches that the men will respond or fail to respond according to what we are in ourselves. [Morgan, 61-62]

### Summary

As we finish this chapter on the Parable of the Sower, let's review what we have learned. In Jesus' explanation of this parable, He gave several reasons why the hard-hearted Israelites had rejected their Messiah and King, resulting in the postponement of the kingdom. Some were overtly hostile to the message, while others succumbed to external or internal pressures. The "word of the kingdom" had been proclaimed to them so that they did hear the message, which included truths about the spiritual qualifications for establishing the kingdom. It required both understanding and accepting Jesus as the Messiah as well as personally turning to God in repentance, which was something the majority of them were quite unwilling to do.

Paraphrasing what Jesus said in Matt 13:13, "This is why I speak to them in parables, because they refuse to perceive and understand." We can see that the Parable of the Sower serves as a transition to the next group of six "kingdom parables" that will share "the mysteries of the kingdom of heaven" which Jesus mentioned in Matt 13:11. As we stated previously, this is a parable about why Jesus began to speak to the multitude in parables.

Many Bible commentaries include this parable with the later ones which share mysteries of the kingdom, but this first parable is an introduction to those parables, rather than giving new revelation about events during the postponement of the kingdom. As one Bible scholar has said, "As far as Matthew 13 is concerned one must look on the parable of the sower and the soils as being introductory and not as containing new revelations concerning the kingdom of heaven. This parable reveals the principle that God gives fruit to those who initially receive and understand the word of the kingdom." [Toussaint-J, 355]

Another issue we sometimes see is that many Bible commentaries limit this parable only to discussing people's responses to the gospel for salvation during the Church Age. One scholar described this tendency while referencing several examples of these interpretations:

> Many Bible commentaries assert that Jesus depicted the responses that four different categories of people will have to the gospel, concluding, "The gospel will be rejected by most people." Some claim that only the last soil portrays a believer because it produces fruit. Others assert that only the first soil type repre-

sents an unbeliever because the seed germinates in the other three. Therefore, the parable is used to evaluate whether people are saved, unsaved, carnal, persevering, or even not saved but think they are. The conflicting interpretations result from classifying the four soils as unbelievers and the seed as the message of the gospel. ... Some scholars designate salvation as the central truth of the parable, not merely an application point. [Hornock, 185, 187]

But as we have seen, the context of this parable does not support such interpretations. As Dr. Morgan expressed it: "This parable, then, has nothing at all to do with the subject of the Christian Church, neither has it anything to do with that of the conversion of individual men. ... The subject of individual regeneration is taken for granted, and the teaching of Christ is not regarding the salvation of individuals." [Morgan, 63]

This parable is about the nation of Israel's response to the word of the kingdom which had been proclaimed by John the Baptist, Jesus, and the disciples when they declared, "Repent, for the kingdom of heaven is at hand!" Following the nation's rejection of their King, the kingdom was no longer mentioned as being "at hand" but its coming would be delayed until a future time when Israel will meet the spiritual qualifications for the kingdom's inauguration.

# The Parable of the Wheat & Tares

## (Matthew 13:24-30, 36-43)

In the first three chapters of this study we discussed the background or context for Jesus' teaching in parables, and we looked at the introductory Parable of the Sower which Jesus told to the multitude while He was teaching from the boat. We then studied Jesus' answer to His disciples' question about why He began teaching this way, followed by Jesus' own explanation for the meaning of that parable. We saw that the Parable of the Sower was a parable Jesus told to communicate why He began teaching the multitude in parables. In Jesus' explanation of that parable, He gave several reasons why the hard-hearted Israelites had rejected their Messiah and King, resulting in the postponement of the kingdom.

Now, starting in Matt 13:24 Jesus turned back to the multitude standing on the shoreline and told them another parable. This is the first parable in the series which is specifically identified as being about the "kingdom of heaven," which we know from our previous study had been rejected by the Israelites and would be postponed until a time when the nation would willingly meet the spiritual qualifications for it to be established.

In this chapter we are going to see Jesus tell the original story to the crowd in verses 24-30, and then we will bring in verses 36-43 in order to see Jesus' own explanation for the meaning of this story. We usually try to move verse-by-verse through a Bible text, but in this case I think it would be helpful to get all of the details for this parable in one chapter. Beginning in this parable, Jesus will start to share some of the "mysteries of the kingdom of heaven" which He promised in Matt 13:11. These are prophetic glimpses into the characteristics of the time period between Israel's rejection of her King and their eventual acceptance of Him at His second coming in glory. With this in mind, let's begin our study of the parable of the wheat and the tares.

**Matt 13:24 - Jesus presented another parable to them, saying, "The kingdom of heaven may be compared to a man who sowed good seed in his field."**

We saw in previous chapters that Jesus had just spent a few minutes speaking privately to His disciples – answering their question about why He taught the crowd only in parables and then briefly explaining the Parable of the Sower to the disciples who were probably with Him in the boat.

Here in the first phrase of this verse we see that "Jesus presented another parable to them." So is He still speaking only to the disciples or has He turned to address the crowd again? The word **presented** is the Greek word *paratithēmi* which means "to place beside." So Jesus is placing this new parable beside the one He had already given to the crowd. The word **another** is the Greek word *allos* which means "another of the same kind as before," so Jesus has turned back to the multitude on the beach and is telling this second story to them.

He began by introducing this parable with the words, "the kingdom of heaven may be **compared** to..." So Jesus is making it quite clear that He has something to teach by way of comparison. This is the Greek word *homoioō* which means "to illustrate by comparison." The point that He wanted to make – the content of His teaching – would be similar to something which appeared within the story that He told to the multitude.

He said, "The kingdom of heaven may be compared to a man who sowed good seed in his field." So, once again, Jesus is using an agricultural metaphor to communicate this truth. Just as in His first parable, here we see a man – the sower – who is scattering good seed in his cultivated field.

What I would like to do now is to skip down to Jesus' private explanation of this phrase so that we can see the original story side by side with Jesus' interpretation of the elements while we go through the narrative. In Matt 13:36 it says that after teaching in the boat Jesus left the crowds and went into the house, where His disciples came to Him and said, "Explain to us the parable of the tares of the field." So here, as before, we see Jesus giving the explanation of the parable only to His disciples, privately.

**Matt 13:37-38a - And He said, "The one who sows the good seed is the Son of Man, and the field is the world; and as for the good seed, these are the sons of the kingdom;"**

We could represent the text of the parable alongside Jesus' explanation in a chart like the one below.

Here we see Jesus identifying specific elements of the parable so that we can begin putting the puzzle pieces together to understand what He wanted to teach when He used this comparison. The man who is seeding his field is the "Son

| Wheat & Tares | Jesus' Interpretation |
|---|---|
| v24 - presented to the multitude | v36 - shared only with the disciples |
| v24 - man sowed good seed in his field | v37 - man = Son of Man<br>v38 - field = the world<br>good seed = sons of the kingdom |

of Man," which was Jesus' primary title for Himself throughout the Gospel of Matthew (see Matt 8:20; 9:6; 10:23; 11:19;
12:8, 32, 40; 16:13, 27-28; 17:9,12, 22; 18:11; 19:28; 20:18, 28;
24:27, 30, 37, 39, 44; 25:31; 26:2, 24, 45, 64).

In verse 38 He explained that the field is the **world**, which
is the Greek word *kosmos* that can mean several things, including "the world system in operation around us; the inhabi-
tants of the earth; the ungodly multitude; or the whole mass
of men alienated from God and therefore hostile to the cause
of Christ." As one commentator has said, "The field is the
world. So we have here the fact established that after Israel
failed, the Word is to go forth into the wide world" [Gae-
belein, 12]. Notice here that the field is not the Kingdom and
not the Church. The Son of Man is seeding the entire world
with "sons of the kingdom," so His children are not limited
only to people within the nation of Israel.

The seed is identified as the sons of the kingdom. As in the
first parable, the seed in this parable equates to people. In
this case the seed represents the sons or children who are
destined for the kingdom. In previous chapters we have seen
that those who understood and accepted Jesus as the Messiah, as well as personally turning to God in repentance, they
are the ones (as it says in Matt 13:12) who "have and to whom
more will be given so they will have an abundance." Their acceptance of God's chosen King opened the way for them to
participate in the coming kingdom. We know that the entire
nation of Israel may have considered themselves to be "sons
of the kingdom," but because of their rejection of the King
and their refusal to meet the spiritual requirements for the
kingdom, only the believing remnant would become actual
"sons of the kingdom" (Matt 8:12).

Just to be clear, the fact that God would broaden His hori-
zons to include the whole world was a truth that was not a secret or mystery. Even from the earliest promise that God gave
to Abraham, the Old Testament had said, "In your seed all the

nations of the earth shall be blessed" (Genesis 12:3; 22:18; 28:14). So up to this point in the parable we have not seen a mystery being revealed. However, it is quite encouraging that, during the period of time when the kingdom is postponed, the Son of Man will include the entire world within the boundaries of His field.

Those who come to faith in Christ during the kingdom's postponement are described in later New Testament revelation as "sons" or "heirs." For example, Gal 4:6-7 says, "Because you are sons, God has sent forth the Spirit of His Son into our hearts, crying, Abba! Father! Therefore you are no longer a slave, but a son; and if a son, then an heir through God." A son and heir is entitled to the inheritance, but he does not yet possess it. 2 Peter 1:10-11 says, "Therefore, brethren, be all the more diligent to make certain about His calling and choosing you; for as long as you practice these things, you will never stumble; for in this way the entrance into the eternal kingdom of our Lord and Savior Jesus Christ will be abundantly supplied to you." Their inheritance of the kingdom was guaranteed, but their entrance into that kingdom will not take place until a future time.

Let's go back to see the next part of the original parable.

**Matt 13:25 - "But while his men were sleeping, his enemy came and sowed tares among the wheat, and went away."**

In His later explanation of the parable, Jesus does not address the first phrase that we see here: "while his men were sleeping." That is because He was simply painting a picture of how the enemy worked during the night when no one was watching. The field workers were supposed to be sleeping at night, so the enemy knew that was a time when he could do his destructive work without being seen. **Enemy** is the Greek word *echthros* which means "a hateful or hostile person; an adversary or foe."

What did this enemy do? He secretly over-sowed the field with tares and then went away. In our culture today, we may not understand how damaging this act of the enemy was, but hopefully it will become clearer as we learn more about tares and how dangerous they are. **Tares** is the Greek word *zizanion* which one commentary said is derived from 'zan' meaning "vomiting." [Pulpit in e-Sword] Some Bible translations use the word darnel instead of tares, and both terms refer to the same plant whose botanical name is *Lolium temulentum*. Eating grains from this plant can produce violent nausea, convulsions, and diarrhea which in some cases resulted in death. So this enemy deliberately tried to ruin the entire crop which the sower was expecting his plants to produce. One classic Middle-East scholar described the situation like this:

> In those parts where the grain has headed out, the tares have done the same, and there a child could not mistake them for wheat or barley; but where both are less developed, the closest scrutiny will often fail to detect them. Even the farmers, who in this country generally weed their fields, do not pretend to distinguish the one from the other until both are well grown. They would not only mistake good grain for tares, but very commonly the roots of the two are so intertwined that it is impossible to separate them without plucking up both. ... The grain is small, and is arranged along the upper part of the stalk, which stands perfectly erect. Its taste is bitter, and when eaten separately, or when diffused in ordinary bread, it causes dizziness, and often acts as an emetic. In short, it is a strong soporific poison, and must be carefully winnowed, and picked out of the wheat, grain by grain, before grinding or the flour is not healthy. Of course the farmers are very anxious to exterminate it, but that is nearly impossible. [Thomson, 395-396]

So, not only do the tares produce grain that is unhealthy, but while they are growing in the field they are almost indistinguishable from the wheat that is growing right beside it. Only after the wheat and tares have both produced heads of grain is it possible to reliably tell the difference. During most of their lifecycle, the bad plants look exactly like the good plants. The tares produce heads of grain that are light in weight so the stalks stand up straight, even after the heads have formed. It is different from wheat, whose heads of grain become heavier so that the stalks bend over more and more as they ripen. This allows the farmer to go through the field during the harvest and to cut the heads off the tares, putting them aside first, so he can then harvest the wheat without contaminating it.

Now, when we turn to Jesus' private explanation to His disciples, we see that He identified the tares and the enemy.

## Matt 13:38b-39a - "the tares are the sons of the evil one; and the enemy who sowed them is the devil"

Just as the good seed represented the "sons of the kingdom," the tares represent the "sons of the evil one."

The enemy is the devil. He is a real, personal spirit being who constantly opposes and seeks to undermine the work of Christ. This is not the first time we have seen the devil mentioned in the Gospel of Matthew. In chapter 4, as Jesus was beginning His public ministry to the nation of Israel it says that "Jesus was led up by the Spirit into the wilderness to be tempted by the devil" (Matt 4:1). From other passages in the Bible we know that Satan exercises authority over the *kosmos* or world system (1 John 5:19). He is called "the god of this world" and can blind people's minds in order to prevent them from becoming believers, according to 2 Cor 4:3-4 which says, "Even if our gospel is veiled, it is veiled to those who are

| Wheat & Tares | Jesus' Interpretation |
|---|---|
| v25 - at night his enemy sowed tares in the field and went away | v38 - tares = sons of the evil one |
| | v39 - enemy = the devil |

perishing, in whose case the god of this world has blinded the minds of the unbelieving so that they might not see the light of the gospel of the glory of Christ, who is the image of God." The devil deceives the nations and can use human authorities to hinder the work of Christ (1 Thess 2:18). To do this, he disguises his servants as servants of righteousness (2 Cor 11:15). One theology reference described his activity this way:

> It is also revealed that Satan in his warfare will counterfeit the things of God, which will be in accord with his purpose to be "like the most High." He will promote extensive religious systems (1 Tim 4:1-3; 2 Cor 11:13-15). In this connection it should be observed that Satan can promote forms of religion which are based on selected Bible texts, which elevate Christ as the leader, and which incorporate every phase of the Christian faith except one – the doctrine of salvation by grace alone on the ground of the shed blood of Christ. Such satanic delusions are now in the world and multitudes are being deceived by them. Such false systems are always to be tested by the attitude they take toward the saving grace of God through the efficacious blood of Christ (Rev 12:11). [MBT, 163]

The phrase "sons of the evil one" refers to people in the world who are under the influence and control of the devil. By comparison then, just as the tares are almost indistinguishable from wheat during all but the last part of their lifecycle, it may be quite difficult to distinguish the "sons of the evil one" from the "sons of the kingdom" as they appear together in the world where they are growing. During the period while the kingdom is postponed, Jesus is telling us that both types of people will be living side by side and that it may be difficult to tell them apart. Satan's counterfeit religious systems may appear to be good and worthwhile to the majority of people living in the world during the time before Jesus returns to establish His kingdom. As one commentator expressed it:

> The Lord Jesus sows seed, so now [Satan] too will sow seed. Remember, Satan is never an innovator but always an imitator. His counterfeits are people, his own attempted reproduction of the people of God. While the Lord is sowing the good seed who are

His children, Satan is sowing tares who are his children. The counterfeit is in appearance so much like the genuine the two are not distinguishable. ... When Satan sows his seed he imitates the good seed. It was to the religious intelligensia, the scribes and Pharisees, that Jesus spoke when He said, "Ye are of your father the devil" (John 8:44). They were the ones upon whom Christ pronounced severe judgment, calling them hypocrites and blind (Matt 23:13-33). ... [A hypocrite] is playing the part of another. Such are the tares in this parable. They are Satan's children presenting themselves as the children of God. [Strauss, 57-58]

So, here in this part of the parable we see that the good plants and the bad plants will grow together throughout this extended period during which the kingdom is postponed. There will be "sons of the evil one" who may outwardly appear to be good and genuine, but who are displaying a false righteousness. One commentator has said, "This parable, then, gives a remarkable exposé of the methods employed by Satan. He seeks to destroy God's testimony on earth by introducing ... a clever imitation of the real thing. And this parable reveals that he works from within: he sowed the tares among the wheat!" [Pink]

When we turn back to Jesus' story given publically to the crowd, He says that it is only after the wheat and tares develop heads of grain that it is possible to tell them apart.

**Matt 13:26 - "But when the wheat sprouted and bore grain, then the tares became evident also."**

Here in Jesus' original story we see that it was not easy to discover what had happened until after the heads of grain had formed and began to ripen. By that time it was too late to prevent the damage, which had actually been done quite some time before the seeds started to sprout. The field workers could finally see the tares with their heads of grain standing straight and tall above the stalks of wheat, which were starting to bend over under the weight of their heads of good grain. This shocking discovery led the field workers to immediately ask the landowner some questions.

**Matt 13:27 - "The slaves of the landowner came and said to him, 'Sir, did you not sow good seed in your field? How then does it have tares?'"**

What we see here is the beginning of a dialog between the field workers and the landowner. These next few verses do not have any corresponding explanation by Jesus. At first glance the workers' question may seem a little harsh. They did start by calling him "Sir," which was a title of respect – but then they said, in essence, "Are you sure you didn't do something wrong here?" One commentator described their response this way:

> The occasion of the conversation is the extreme surprise of the servants at the appearance of the darnel. They know, or at least assume, that their master sowed good, exclusively good, grain in his field. And yet amid the good grain they find the darnel grown so thickly, that it can only have been sown on purpose. [Goebel, 60]

So, to the workers, the situation they discovered in the field seemed almost beyond comprehension. They could think of no reasonable explanation for what they discovered as they surveyed the wheat field.

**Matt 13:28 - "And he said to them, 'An enemy has done this!' The slaves said to him, 'Do you want us, then, to go and gather them up?'"**

The landowner's response showed that he was not responsible, but that this situation must have been the act of someone hostile to him. Notice that the landowner said, "An enemy has done this!" Not "the enemy" or "my enemy." Since it had been a secret attack, he had no way of knowing for sure who was responsible. But he could clearly see that over-sowing his field with tares was a hostile and spiteful attack which would only be done by someone who deliberately intended to

The discovery of the tares among the wheat.

do him harm.

The servants reacted to this news with a strong desire to solve the problem. They asked whether they should immediately remove the tares – forgetting for the moment that by that time the roots of both plants would have become inseparable. Unfortunately, getting rid of the tares would probably result in the loss of the entire crop since the whole field had been over-sown.

**Matt 13:29 - "But he said, 'No; for while you are gathering up the tares, you may uproot the wheat with them.'"**

First, the landowner reminded the workers that gathering the tares would mean losing the wheat, too. This would have been an extreme option for dealing with the problem. They could pull up everything or even burn the field, but that would mean accepting a total loss of that year's crop. However, the landowner was not willing to accept the loss if there might be a chance of saving the good grain.

**Matt 13:30 - "Allow both to grow together until the harvest; and in the time of the harvest I will say to the reapers, 'First gather up the tares and bind them in bundles to burn them up; but gather the wheat into my barn.'"**

Here the landowner gives his decision to his workers. They are to allow the good and bad plants to continue growing side by side until the end of their lifecycle, at which time the reapers would then be called to gather the harvest. At that time the landowner would give special instructions to the reapers about how to deal with the mixed crop. He will tell them to gather the tares first. Because their stalks stand straight and tall, they will be easier to distinguish from the wheat. The tares would be bundled and then set aside so they could be dealt with later. Finally, the reapers would gather the wheat normally and bring it into the barn or granary. After the good crop is safely in the storehouse, the landowner would be free to deal with the tares.

Here in verse 30 we come to the end of the parable that Jesus told to the multitude while He was teaching from the boat. In the rest of our study we will finish by looking at the rest of Jesus' explanation to His disciples about the meaning of the story. So, Jesus will pick up the storyline at this point in the narrative and He will give additional information as part of His private explanation of the parable.

## Matt 13:39b - and the harvest is the end of the age; and the reapers are angels.

At the end of this verse Jesus tells us that the time of the final harvest equates to the end of the age. **Age** is the Greek word *aiōn* which indicates an extended, unbroken period of time. And **end** is the Greek word *sunteleia* which means "to bring everything together in completion or consummation." This is the same phrase that is used in Matt 24:3, which says, "As He was sitting on the Mount of Olives, the disciples came to Him privately, saying, 'Tell us, when will these things happen, and what will be the sign of Your coming, and of the end of the age?'" So, it seems like the disciples clearly remembered what Jesus said when He used the phrase "the end of the age" here in His explanation of this parable. They knew that He was talking about a time in the distant future when the "sons of the kingdom" will be separated from the "sons of the evil one" at the return of the King to establish His kingdom.

One commentator summarized the situation at this point in the parable when he said,

> The devil's method is that of mingling the counterfeit with the real. It is that of introducing into the Master's own property that which is so like the good that at first you cannot tell the difference. That is the devil's mission of imitation. It is the heart of the parable. What is to be the issue of the two sowings? Their time of operation is to be until "the end of the age," and until then the word of the King is, "'Let both grow together until the harvest." Let these two sowings work themselves out to final manifestation, and then there will be separation. [Morgan, 84]

Now, in this parable, the workers would only have to wait for a few weeks or months in order for that season's harvest to arrive. But in the comparison which Jesus is making, He is saying that we must wait for an extended period of time, until a "harvest" in the distant future when the good will be separated from the bad. We also see at the end of verse 39 that Jesus identified the reapers as angels. We can keep this fact in mind as we look for the involvement of angels in the fulfillment of that coming harvest.

**Matt 13:40 - "So just as the tares are gathered up and burned with fire, so shall it be at the end of the age."**

Jesus is obviously using the language of comparison in this verse. He says that "just as" in His original story the next step would be the burning of the bundles of tares, so it will be at the end of the age. Since Jesus equated the tares to be "sons of the evil one," we could substitute "sons of the evil one" for tares in this sentence, and the verse could be paraphrased this way: "At the end of the age the sons of the evil one will be gathered up and burned with fire." This clearly presents a picture of the final judgment of these wicked ones.

In the next verse Jesus goes on to provide details about who will do the gathering, as well as what characterizes these "sons of the evil one."

**Matt 13:41 - "The Son of Man will send forth His angels, and they will gather out of His kingdom all stumbling blocks, and those who commit lawlessness,"**

We know from verse 39 that the reapers from the parable are actually angels who will carry out the instructions of the Master at the future harvest. Christ will not use men to carry out this task. Instead He will assign His angels to do this work. He says that they will gather them "out of His kingdom." This does not mean that any of the "sons of the evil one" will be participants in His kingdom. One Greek language scholar explained it this way:

> What this means is that, just as the wheat and the darnel are mixed together in the field till the separation at harvest, so the evil are mixed with the good in the world (the field). Jesus does not mean to say that these "stumbling-blocks" are actually in the Kingdom of heaven and really members of the Kingdom. They

are simply mixed in the field with the wheat and God leaves them in the world till the separation comes. [Robertson in e-Sword]

This separation will occur at the time during which Jesus begins to set up His kingdom on earth.

In the last part of this verse we see two characteristics of the "sons of the evil one." First, they are called **stumbling blocks**, and this is from the Greek word *skandalon* from which we get our English word "scandal." It means someone "who causes ruin, destruction, or misery; or someone who is the cause or occasion for sinning." Second, the "sons of the evil one" are described as "those who commit lawlessness." **Lawlessness** is the Greek word *anomia* which means to live apart from the law, to violate the law, or to be unrighteous. As it says in 1 Cor 6:9, "Do you not know that the unrighteous will not inherit the kingdom of God?" There is no place for the unrighteous in Christ's kingdom and they will never enter it.

Jesus then goes on to explain what will happen to both the "sons of the evil one" and the "sons of the kingdom." The angels will gather the "sons of the evil one" ...

**Matt 13:42-43 - "and will throw them into the furnace of fire; in that place there will be weeping and gnashing of teeth. Then THE RIGHTEOUS WILL SHINE FORTH AS THE SUN in the kingdom of their Father. He who has ears, let him hear."**

According to the word picture Jesus has been painting for us, the "sons of the kingdom" and the "sons of the evil one" will be living in the world throughout the age. The judgment event that Jesus described here in His explanation of this parable to His disciples, will happen at a time when these two types of people are both alive on earth, and it will occur at the end of the age when Jesus comes to establish His earthly kingdom. This description is very much like what Jesus would later tell His disciples shortly before His crucifixion. Jesus' prophecy in Matt 25:31-46 is often titled the "Sheep and Goats Judgment" because there He was using an illustration from animal husbandry. But the sheep are analogous to the wheat in our Matt 13 parable, while the goats are the same as the tares.

In Matt 25 Jesus would tell them: "When the Son of Man comes in His glory, and all the angels with Him, then He will sit on His glorious throne. All the nations will be gathered before Him; and He will separate them from one another, as the shepherd separates the sheep from the goats; and He will put the sheep on His right, and the goats on the left. Then the King will say to those on His right, 'Come, you who are blessed of My Father, inherit the kingdom prepared for you from the foundation of the world.' (Matt 25:31-34) ... Then He will also say to those on His left, 'Depart from Me, accursed ones, into the eternal fire which has been prepared for the devil and his angels'" (Matt 25:41).

This judgment that Jesus prophesied will occur after the future seven-year Tribulation, and it is a judgment of living people who survive that horrific event. At that time Jesus will separate the sheep from the goats – the wheat from the tares. Here in Matt 13 what we have is a preview in parable form of the prophecy that Jesus shared in Matt 25. The "sons of the evil one" will be thrown into the furnace of fire where there will be weeping and gnashing of teeth. But the "sons of the kingdom" will shine forth as the sun in the kingdom of their Father. One commentator well expresses a sense of expectation and gratitude for the coming end of the age when he says,

> There is a day coming, thank God, when this age shall end. The age is necessary, but preliminary only, and it is at last to be consummated. The history of the world will not end with the consummation of this age. There is to be another age ushered in by the burning of the darnel and the garnering of the wheat, an age

which shall be initiated by the King's clearing out of His field all the things which offend. [Morgan, 87-88]

## Summary

As we end this chapter on the Parable of the Wheat & Tares, let's review what Jesus taught about the mysteries of the coming kingdom.

First, there would be a long period of time between Jesus' rejection as King and His eventual coming in glory. This was a truth that had not been previously revealed in the Old Testament. A new age must come before the millennial kingdom is inaugurated. As one scholar has said:

> The parable of the tares explains to the disciples that, in spite of the rejection of Christ by the current leaders of Israel, the promises and expectations about the coming kingdom would be fulfilled as God had said. However, before that time comes, some other events will take place relative to and in preparation for that kingdom. It is these events and the time frame associated with it that is the mystery unknown in the past and now being revealed in the kingdom parables. [Stallard, 344]

So, even though the kingdom of heaven had been rejected by the nation of Israel and its coming was postponed, there will still be "sons of the kingdom" – those who will eventually claim their inheritance and assume their place in the kingdom – and they will populate the world during the entire interval while the coming of the kingdom is delayed.

Second, the Lord's disciples and all true "sons of the kingdom" have wanted to know when the kingdom would come. Here in this parable Jesus teaches that the kingdom will be established at the "end of the age." As one definitive, classic study of the kingdom puts it,

> His hearers desire to know when it will be established. ... This parable locates the establishment of the kingdom at the period of the harvest. To obtain the force of the parable it is requisite to supply the idea of the setting up of the kingdom as to manner and time and then to notice what things Jesus teaches are re-

quired before this will be done. The kingdom is not likened to any particular one thing in the parable but to the final result, the end. ... It is not likened to a man, or to his acts, or to the good seed which grows into wheat, or to the field which is the world, or to the tares which are mixed with the wheat, or even to the harvest; but all these are used to indicate how certain things must be accomplished until the end of the age, when the righteous, the gathered wheat, shall shine forth as the sun in the kingdom. [Peters, 21]

Third, Jesus illustrated in this parable that the "sons of the kingdom" will live side by side with "sons of the evil one" throughout this intervening time period. This tells us that we should not be taken completely by surprise when we hear about "tares" among the "wheat." An inner sense of righteousness and justice within every "son of the kingdom" may cry out, "This should not be!" But our Lord has told us that there will be "false wheat" mingled with the good seed during this age. One thing we must keep in mind is that "Sons of the kingdom" exist both before and after the Church Age. Matthew 13 is not dealing specifically with the Church, since the interim age extends well beyond the time between Pentecost and the Rapture. One writer has clarified this truth, while at the same time explaining our responsibility within the Church during this time:

> The field is the world, not the church. We cannot keep the world pure from these kinds of people, but we can certainly do everything within our power to keep the church as pure as possible and free from immorality and doctrinal error. Church leaders cannot remove those with doctrinal or moral problems from the world, but they can excommunicate them from the local assembly, when the Word of God calls for such action. [Middletown, 13]

The existence of "sons of the evil one" within the world can only be remedied at the coming of Christ to set up His millennial kingdom. As one commentator expressed it,

In this age that shall span the time between the rejection of the King and His return, the sons of the kingdom shall exist side by side with the sons of the evil one. At the time the King returns and manifests His Kingdom, the tares shall be gathered out and the wheat shall be ushered in. ... It is when the King is sitting on His throne that all nations are gathered before Him and He separates the sheep and the goats. [Benson, 11]

Fourth, in his desire to "be like God," the devil, the enemy of the Son of Man, seeks to be worshiped as God. To accomplish this, he will create all kinds of false religious systems which he can use to deceive human beings into worshiping him rather than the only true God. As one commentator has said, "Satan's biggest operation is in religion." [Strauss, 58] Throughout the age there will be a wide variety of so-called "spiritual" groups that the devil will use to lead people away from the one true God (1 Tim 4:1-2; 2 Tim 3:2-6; 2 Pet 2:1-3; 2 John 1:7-11; Jude 1:4). There will be a wide range of options – some are completely pagan or animistic, some are occult or practice mysticism, while some are pseudo-Christian groups.

I would like to share one final quote before we close this chapter. Many "sons of the kingdom" have wondered why God allows the devil seemingly to have free reign during this interim age. One commentator shares an insight which puts the issue in perspective:

This is a point which has perplexed many. Why did the Lord permit the enemy to sow his tares? And why has He permitted them for so long, to occupy the principal part of the field? In other words, Why has God allowed the devil such long-continued freedom? This is not so difficult to answer as many may suppose. They overlook the fact that the leaders of this world rejected its rightful Sovereign; that the Jews preferred Barabbas. Having chosen a murderer in preference to the Lord of Life, both Jews and Gentiles have reaped what they sowed. The devil was "a murderer from the beginning" (John 8:14), and having refused the Savior, this great soul-destroyer has ruled over them ever since! [Pink]

# The Mustard Seed & the Leaven

## (Matthew 13:31-35)

In the last chapter we discussed the Parable of the Wheat & Tares, which was the first parable in the series specifically identified as being about the "kingdom of heaven." In that parable, Jesus began to share some of the "mysteries of the kingdom" which He had promised in Matt 13:11. These are prophetic glimpses into the characteristics of the time period between Israel's rejection of her King and their eventual acceptance of Him at His second coming in glory.

In the Parable of the Wheat & Tares Jesus said, "The kingdom of heaven may be compared to a man who sowed good seed in his field." The man was identified as the "Son of Man" and the field is the world. There were two main lessons from the Parable of the Wheat & Tares. First, the kingdom would not come until the harvest at the "end of the age." Second, there would be good seed and bad seed which would grow side by side until the end of the growing season.

In this chapter we will be discussing the next two parables that Jesus gave to the multitude on the beach as He taught from the boat. Just as He did when He shared the Parable of the Wheat & Tares, Jesus did not provide any explanation of the parables when He was speaking to the crowd. It was only when Jesus retreated into the house that He shared an explanation of the Parable of the Wheat & Tares privately with His disciples. In the two brief parables we will discuss today, Jesus did not give any interpretation at all – either to the crowd or to His disciples.

Because Jesus did not give an explanation for the intended meaning of these parables, our task of interpreting them is much more challenging. One thing we know is that the meaning of these parables was clear in the mind of Jesus. He knew exactly what He intended to illustrate with these word pictures. But one thing we cannot do is to insert our own meanings into these parables. Since Jesus did not explicitly tell us what He was thinking, we need to rely on the context for clues that will help us determine His meaning. Ultimately we should not say anything beyond what is justified by the text of the parables. It is always safer to state what the text says, rather than venturing into speculation which might add meanings that Jesus never intended.

There are several rules of interpretation that will help us. First, "Context is King." Even if the meaning of a Bible passage is unclear, often the immediate context of the unclear passage will shed light on its meaning. Second, "Scripture interprets Scripture." When we come across a Bible passage that is unclear, there may be a similar idea in a similar context that can shed light on the meaning of the unclear passage. Third, "What does the text say?" In other words, Scripture itself is our sole authority, and we should be cautious whenever we try to use our own flawed human logic to make inferences about the meaning of unclear passages. As one scholar expressed it:

> Rational powers are God-given, and our commission is to study thoroughly so that we may correctly handle the Word of God with no need to be ashamed. ... Since revelation is limited...it may be legitimate to logically deduce the missing elements. But if Scripture is our sole authority, we may not invest [our own] logical deductions with divine authority. ... Most of the great controversies on Christian doctrine have grown out of attempts to define what is left undefined in Scripture. [McQuilkin, 235]

I think that is very wise counsel from a seasoned Bible interpreter. In the case of today's two unexplained parables of the kingdom, we will study their immediate context as well as looking at a cross-reference from a similar context in the book of Matthew that might help us to determine the meaning. But when all is said and done, there may be aspects of these unexplained parables that we must simply hold in an open hand – allowing God to have His mysteries, and (with gratefulness) being content with the sure Word of truth that God has permitted us to understand.

One commentator has this to say about our approach to these two parables:

> We must be suspicious of any interpretation of the one parable which contradicts that of any other. We may take it for granted that Christ is consistent in His teaching. Hence the value of the fact that the first two parables were explained by the King Himself. From these explanations we may proceed to an examination of all the rest. Once again, we must remember the consistency of our Lord's figures. He does not confuse them in His use. The sower of the different parables always represents the same person, and so throughout. When He has given us the explanation of a figure we may apply that explanation uniformly. [Morgan, 94]

Since Jesus gave all of these parables in one sitting, we can be confident that the elements of His overall message will be consistent rather than contradictory. The parables of the Mustard Seed and the Leaven appear in the immediate context where Jesus was illustrating some of the "mysteries of the kingdom" for the multitude. He explained the first of these parables – the Parable of the Wheat & Tares – privately to His disciples, so we should use that first "kingdom parable" and its explanation as the pattern for interpreting the two unexplained parables which Jesus gave to the crowd.

With all of this in mind, let's begin looking at the Parable of the Mustard Seed.

**Matt 13:31 - He presented another parable to them, saying, "The kingdom of heaven is like a mustard seed, which a man took and sowed in his field;"**

We see here that Jesus is still teaching from the boat and addressing the multitude who stood on the beach. In this new parable, Jesus is making a comparison that uses another illustration from agriculture. The story tells of a man who took a mustard seed and sowed or planted it in his field. Notice that he plants a single mustard seed, since the Greek word for **seed** (*kokkos*) is singular in number. This is not the picture of a man scattering handfuls of seed across his plowed field. What we see here is more like a gardener who takes an individual seed and carefully plants it in an herb pot or in a prepared garden bed. Jesus goes on to say ...

**Matt 13:32 - "and this is smaller than all other seeds, but when it is full grown, it is larger than the garden plants and becomes a tree, so that THE BIRDS OF THE AIR come and NEST IN ITS BRANCHES."**

A mustard seed is extremely tiny. When Jesus says that it was "smaller than all other seeds" He is obviously referring to all of the other common garden plants that were familiar to the people He was speaking to on the shoreline. One of the keys to interpreting this parable will be to learn more about the mustard plant that Jesus was referring to. Just as it was important to understand the characteristics of the specific plants involved in the Parable of the Wheat & Tares, the same is true in this parable. The normal characteristics of the common mustard plant hold the key for interpreting the parable. A standard Bible plant reference has this to say about the mustard plant:

> There has been much discussion and argument as to what the mustard plant of Jesus' parables really was. The Greek word in the original texts is *sinapi*. Most modern commentators agree that it was the ordinary black mustard, Brassica nigra. This plant is extensively cultivated for its seeds, which are not only ground up to produce the mustard paste, but also yield a useful oil similar to colza oil. ... While these mustards do not usually grow more than 3 or 4 feet tall, plants have been found to be 10 and

The full-grown mustard tree at the time of the harvest.

even 15 feet tall, with a main stem as thick as a man's arm. Although they are only annual plants, their stems and branches in
autumn become hard and rigid and of quite sufficient strength
to bear the weight of small birds that are attracted by the edible
seeds. ... It is perhaps worthy of note that the seeds of Brassica
are small, and were probably the smallest seeds known to the
common country folk comprising Jesus' audience in Galilee. ...
Brassica nigra did become one of the largest annual herbs in the
region. ... Some commentators are of the opinion that the passage implies that birds built their nests in the branches of the
mustard. The Greek word employed has no such connotation; it
merely means "to settle or rest upon." ... Nor is it justified to
suppose that the expression "fowls of the air" denotes large and
heavy chicken-like or hawk-like birds. It seems most probable
that the word was used to denote the common insessorial
(perching) birds of the region, like linnets and finches. Small
sparrow-like birds perched on the branches of the mature mus-

tard plants in order to eat the seeds in the ripening pods. [Moldenke, 59, 61]

Jesus could have chosen any number of plants for this parable, but He chose the mustard plant for a specific reason. First of all, the characteristics of this common plant were well-known to His listeners. He is not relying on some mysterious or secret quality of this plant in order to make His point. Everyone knew how small the mustard seeds were. In fact, Jesus used the small size of these seeds in order to make a different point in Matt 17:20 when He said to them, "Truly I say to you, if you have faith the size of a mustard seed, you will say to this mountain, 'Move from here to there,' and it will move; and nothing will be impossible to you." So, the small size of mustard seeds was common knowledge.

Another aspect of the mustard plant that was common knowledge was that it grew very quickly to become a small bush within just a few weeks, and by the end of the growing season some mustard plants could grow to a height of 10 or 15 feet. The engraving on the previous page is from a 17th century Bible, and it shows a mustard plant that is typical of the one Jesus was talking about. He said, "when it is full grown, it is larger than the **garden plants**" (*lachanon*). This is the common word for a potted herb. So the mustard plant in Jesus' parable was the familiar garden plant that had characteristics which were well known to the people in His audience. There are at least four of these characteristics that are important for interpreting this parable.

- The mustard plant had very small seeds.
- It was an annual plant that could grow to a large size by the end of the growing season. As one expositor has said, "Although belonging to the class of herbs, it becomes a plant like a tree." [Goebel, 95]
- When fully grown it produced seed pods that attracted all kinds of small birds. Birds (*peteinon*) can represent any winged creature, and the most common birds of that region

were small finches and sparrows whose main food was seeds.

– At the end of the annual growing season the seeds would be harvested to make useful products for both food and medicine.

Out of all the possible plants that Jesus could have chosen, the mustard plant was probably the best example to illustrate the striking contrast between the small beginning and the large result within a single growing season. As one scholar expressed it,

Here, therefore, what is pictured is not a field of wheat developing from the seed to ripe fruit, as in the first parables, but the process of growth of a mustard plant. And the peculiarity pointed out in the growth of such a plant consists, on the one hand, in the diminutive smallness of the mustard grain, which has passed into a proverb, and on the other hand in the astonishing, tree-like magnitude of the plant springing from it, a magnitude excelling that of all plants of like kind.
[Goebel, 96-97]

The NAS95 Bible says the birds would nest in the branches. The word for **nest** is the Greek word *kataskēnoō* which means "to rest, live, or settle among the branches." **Branches** (*klados*) are shoots or twigs, so this language does not require the branches to be very large. And the mustard plant does not become something different than or outside of its original nature. Some commentators claim that this mustard seed morphed into something else entirely. For example, one writer has said,

That which Christ here describes is a monstrosity. We are aware that this is denied by some, but our Lord's own words are final. He tells us that when this mustard seed is grown it is the "greatest among herbs, and becomes a tree" (v. 32). "Herbs" are an entirely different specie from trees. That which distinguished them is that their stems never develop woody tissue, but live only long enough for the development of flowers and seeds. But this "herb" became a "tree;" that is to say, it developed into something entirely foreign to its very nature and constitution. [Pink]

This comment seems to take the growth of the mustard plant beyond what is warranted by Jesus' description in the text. In order to avoid extremes it seems best to stay within the realm of the facts that Jesus' audience would have known about the common mustard plant.

There are other commentaries that emphasize the size of the tree, as if the mustard plant became a mighty spreading oak or cedar. Several Old Testament passages do use the metaphor of a large spreading tree with birds flocking to its branches to illustrate a kingdom that is perceived as great and powerful (Judges 9:15; Ezekiel 17:22-24; 31:3-14; Daniel 4:7-23). However, we should use caution when appealing to cross-references from different contexts in Scripture in an effort to justify an interpretation of a particular passage. As seminary professors often say, "A text without a context is a pretext for a prooftext." But, based on these types of cross-references, many commentators claim that the Parable of the Mustard Seed pictures a powerful worldly empire of Christendom which develops during the inter-advent age. For example, one writer has said,

> In the parable of the mustard seed, the tree symbolizes growth, greatness, and prominence. Judged by the world's standards, its size and influence make it important so that now it is popular to find shelter in this religious monstrosity. Even the worldly and wealthy are being drawn to it. We can see here a kingdom spreading and flourishing, but it is not the kingdom of God. ... I can think of no better descriptive term for this religious abnormality than Christendom. It is not Christianity; it is an imitation of Christianity, but it is religious. [Strauss, 63, 69]

Now, is it true that religious apostasy will run rampant in the last days? Yes, this is absolutely true, and there are many Bible passages which describe the development of this coming apostasy (2 Thess 2:3-12; 1 Tim 4:1-3; 2 Tim 3:1-7, 4:3-4; 2 Pet 2:1-3, 3:3-4; Rev 17). But, although there is quite a bit of later New Testament revelation about the last days apostasy of the Church and the false religious system established by the devil during the end times, I (for one) am not comfortable reading all of that later revelation back into Jesus' Parable of the Mustard Seed. Is it possible that Jesus was prefiguring those later truths in this parable? I suppose it is possible, but I don't see evidence in the text itself to support such an interpretation of the parable.

One other aspect of the Parable of the Mustard Seed that many commentators emphasize is the symbolism of the birds. Typically these commentators represent the birds from the previous Parable of the Wheat & Tares as "agents of the devil" who snatch up the gospel from unresponsive hearts. In an attempt to apply the elements of the parables consistently, they then identify the birds resting in the mustard tree as "agents of evil" too. One writer stated:

> But we do not have to go outside of Matthew 13 itself to discover what Christ referred to under the figure of these "birds." The Greek word in verse 32 is precisely the same as that which is rendered "birds" in verse 4, which are explained in verse 19 as "the wicked." How, then, can this great "tree" represent the true Church of Christ, while its branches afford shelter for the Devil and his emissaries? ... Satan now moved worldly men to seek membership in the churches of God. These soon caused the Truth to be watered down, discipline to be relaxed, that which repelled the world to be kept in the background, and what would appeal to the carnal mind to be made prominent. Instead of affections being set upon things above, they were fixed on things below. Soon Christianity ceased to be hated by the unregenerate: the gulf between the world and the "Church" was bridged. [Pink]

Again, I ask myself, is this description true, both of the Church today as well as of what it is predicted to become in the last days? Yes, this description is absolutely true, and we could refer to the Bible passages listed earlier to confirm that all of this is true. But, as I mentioned before, I personally don't believe there is evidence in the text itself to indicate that this is what Jesus intended to communicate in this brief story. Are the birds symbolic of "evil" or are they simply behaving as normal seed-eating birds? We know that birds typically look for their food in fields where seeds lay exposed on the ground, or in bushes and trees which have produced seed pods at the time of the harvest. One scholar expressed the issue this way:

> This picture of "birds" and a "tree" to symbolize something evil is not a consistent pattern in Scripture. The examples often cited (Daniel 4:11-12; Ezekiel 31:6) do indeed depict great pagan kingdoms of the earth (i.e. Babylon and Assyria), but the stress seems to be more upon the greatness and scope of these kingdoms rather than upon the evil character thereof. The conclusive proof of this assumption is found in Ezekiel 17:22–24. Note how closely this description of the Messianic kingdom parallels the parable of the mustard seed. ... Thus the figure of birds or of the tree here does not demand an evil or sinister interpretation. The Lord may very well have had this passage in mind as he delivered the parable. [Benson, 12-13]

So, a garden tree where birds are active doesn't necessarily represent anything other than what is described in the text. The birds are behaving exactly as we would expect birds to behave. As was mentioned previously, if Scripture itself is our sole authority, then we should be cautious whenever we attempt to make inferences about the meaning of elements in parables that have not been explicitly interpreted for us by Jesus.

One example of the most common interpretation of the Parable of the Mustard Seed is expressed by this commentator who said, "The kingdom of heaven, though now very small and seemingly insignificant, would one day grow into a large body of believers. That is the central lesson of this parable. ... His kingdom on earth was, figuratively, and relatively speaking, much smaller even than a mustard seed. But the kingdom that started very small would one day become very large." [MacArthur, 370] Another writer has said, "The scope of this parable is to show that the beginnings of the gospel would be small, but that its latter end would greatly increase.

In this way the gospel church, the kingdom of God among us, would be set up in the world." [Matthew Henry in e-Sword]

The majority of modern commentators equate the growth of the mustard plant with the progress of the gospel or the kingdom in the world during the present age. But we should remember that the kingdom of heaven was rejected by the nation of Israel and that these parables deal with the intervening age during which the establishment of the kingdom is delayed. We have God's promise that the kingdom will be a future reality, but it is not in existence today. Jesus did not establish His kingdom – not even in some kind of spiritual or "mystery" form in the present age.

So what can we appeal to for an explanation of the Parable of the Mustard Seed? What information do we have from the context that will help us to determine the meaning which Jesus intended to communicate? As was mentioned previously, since Jesus did not explain the meaning of this parable, we need to go back to the first "kingdom parable," the one that He did explain, in order to find clues to help us determine His meaning. One Bible scholar has expressed it this way:

> The controlling factor here is the parable of the tares, whose presentation introduces the group of three parables and whose interpretation concludes them. That parable has two key elements with respect to the activities of the present time, one good and one evil. It is not a stretch exegetically to see that Jesus gives these two parables (mustard seed and leaven) to illustrate the two elements of good and evil. In this light, the period leading up to the kingdom will see many come to Christ, but will also see many reject Him as well. Each of the two parables illustrates one-half of the description given by the parable of the tares. [Stallard, 353]

The main message from the Parable of the Wheat & Tares was that the kingdom would not come until the time of harvest at the "end of the age." When we look at the Parable of the Mustard Seed that is exactly what we see here, too. Jesus illustrated this truth using a tiny seed which was familiar to

His audience, that when fully grown became a small tree where the birds could perch and where they could feed on the seed pods which had ripened for the harvest. This explanation seems to be the most likely meaning for the Parable of the Mustard Seed.

If we want to see Scriptural support for this interpretation, we can review the other statements of Jesus in the Gospel of Matthew, especially those in which He used the metaphor of a tree to illustrate His point. For example, in Matt 24:32-33 He said, "Now learn the parable from the fig tree: when its branch has already become tender and puts forth its leaves, you know that summer is near; so, you too, when you see all these things, recognize that He is near, right at the door." In that context Jesus was talking about the end of the age and His coming to establish the kingdom, which is almost identical to the context of the Parable of the Mustard Seed.

It seems clear that in the Parable of the Mustard Seed Jesus is teaching a similar truth. Just as when using the characteristics of a fig tree to predict the coming of summer, the same thing applies to the mustard plant. When you see it fully grown with the birds perching in its branches while they feed on its seed pods, you know that the end of the season is near. We might paraphrase this possible interpretation of Jesus' parable by saying, "So, you too, when you see the gathering birds and the ripe pods on the mustard tree, recognize that He is near – that the time for the kingdom to be established is right at the door."

As in the previous parable, in this parable we see something that starts seemingly insignificantly, like the beginning of the age after Jesus' rejection as Messiah and the postponement of the kingdom. But over the course of time, the progress of this age continues until it finally reaches the end of the growing season. At that time the harvest will occur and the ripe seed pods will be gathered. We also know from the Parable of the Wheat & Tares that at that time Jesus will

78

judge the nations and He will inaugurate His kingdom. This seems to be the clearest interpretation for the Parable of the Mustard Seed, and it is also consistent with the message of the Parable of the Wheat & Tares.

Next, Jesus went on to tell one more "kingdom parable" to the multitude gathered along the shoreline.

**Matt 13:33 - He spoke another parable to them, "The kingdom of heaven is like leaven, which a woman took and hid in three pecks of flour until it was all leavened."**

The word **leaven** is the Greek word *zumē* which comes from the word *zeō*, meaning "to be hot or to boil." *Zumē*, then, means to ferment, picturing the bubbling effect of a leavening agent such as yeast in the dough. Leaven has been commonly used in households throughout the world, so the way it worked would have been common knowledge to Jesus' audience. He said that a woman took the leaven and hid it in the milled grain or flour. This pictured the common practice of a woman going about the daily task of making dough and baking bread.

Jesus said that the woman used "three pecks of flour." A **peck** translates the Greek word *saton* which was a dry measure probably equal to about 3 gallons or 14 liters in modern terms. This is probably the same amount of flour that Sarah used as she made bread for Abraham when the LORD appeared to him by the oaks of Mamre (Gen 18:6). One commentator has said, "Three measures of meal would be about 40 litres, which would make enough bread for a meal for 100 people, a remarkable baking for an ordinary woman, but it makes the point vividly!" [France, 227]

We see that the woman **hid** leaven in the flour, and this is the Greek word *egkruptō* which is where we get our English word "encryption." It can mean "to conceal or hide" as well as simply "to mix or to mingle one thing with another." So the

A woman mixing leaven with the dough.

use of this word may not indicate anything beyond the normal process of mixing leaven into a large batch of dough.

As we seek to understand the meaning of this parable, the main element we see is the leaven. Many commentators have struggled to determine whether the leaven in this parable represents something good or something evil, and there is about a 50/50 split in opinion. One scholar has said, "Many contend that the leaven is used here in a good sense and pictures the spread of the gospel throughout the earth. Others state that the word represents evil and is used to illustrate the growth of evil within the group which professes to inherit the kingdom. This latter interpretation has the strongest support." [Toussaint-B, 182]

When we look at the sayings of Jesus in the Gospels we see that He used "leaven" only in a negative sense. He constantly warned His disciples to beware of the "leaven" of the Pharisees, the Sadducees, and Herod. As one commentator has said, "The immediate context supports an understanding of the parable of the leaven as...in harmony with Matthew's association of the term leaven with the evil of the scribes and Pharisees (Matt. 16:6-12)." [Stallard, 353] Also, we see in later New Testament revelation that the apostle Paul used "leaven" solely in a negative sense (1 Cor 5:6-8; Gal 5:7-10). So evidence from the context lends support for the use of "leaven" with a connotation of evil or corruption.

Here in the Parable of the Leaven we see another small beginning with the introduction of a piece of leaven into a very large batch of flour. Then over the course of time, the progress of the age continues until the dough finally reaches the state where (as Jesus said) "it was all leavened." The condition of the fully leavened dough is comparable to the state of the full grown mustard plant, as well as to the status of the harvest of the wheat and tares. In each case, the end of the growing season had finally come.

As we mentioned previously concerning the Parable of the Wheat & Tares, a second important truth was that the good and bad seed would grow side by side until the time of the harvest. Similarly, here in the Parable of the Leaven it seems that there is also a corrupting influence which spreads through the dough over time. One commentator expressed it this way: "This parable reveals the fact that evil will run its course and dominate the new age. But it also indicates that when the program of evil has been fulfilled, the kingdom will come." [Toussaint-B, 182]

So, like the Parable of the Wheat & Tares as well as the Parable of the Mustard Seed, in the Parable of the Leaven Jesus illustrated the period of time between Israel's rejection of their King and His eventual return at the end of the age to establish His kingdom. This intervening time would be characterized by the growth of both the good and the bad over the course of the age. When the end of the season finally comes, there will be a judgment event followed by the establishment of the kingdom by the glorified King.

**Matt 13:34 - All these things Jesus spoke to the crowds in parables, and He did not speak to them without a parable.**

At the end of this section Matthew gave a brief statement concerning Jesus' use of parables to teach the multitude. This verse and the one that follows are a fitting conclusion for Jesus' public teaching to the people on shore while He was sitting in the boat that day. Matthew tells us that during this entire sermon Jesus spoke to the crowd only in parables. In the second chapter we discussed the reason why Jesus taught the multitude using only parables. Here in this verse Matthew confirms this is exactly the method Jesus used that day, and which He would continue to use in His public ministry because of Israel's rejection of Him as their Messiah and King.

**Matt 13:35 - This was to fulfill what was spoken through the prophet: "I WILL OPEN MY MOUTH IN PARABLES; I WILL UTTER THINGS HIDDEN SINCE THE FOUNDATION OF THE WORLD."**

Here in this verse Matthew tells us that Jesus' teaching in parables corresponded to what the psalmist Asaph wrote in Psalm 78:2. We might say that what Asaph wrote in that psalm was well suited to describe Jesus' teaching method to the multitudes. Here Matthew identified Asaph as a prophet, and we see this fact confirmed in 1 Chron 25:2 where it says that Asaph "prophesied under the direction of the king."

The first phrase, "I will open my mouth in parables," is almost identical to the wording in the Greek translation of the Hebrew text (LXX). The second phrase, "I will utter things hidden since the foundation of the world," is an expanded version of the Septuagint text. Here under the inspiration of the Holy Spirit, Matthew elaborated on the words of Asaph in order to emphasize that Jesus was sharing "mysteries of the kingdom of heaven" as it says in Matt 13:11. This helps us to understand that those mysteries were indeed some of the secret, eternal counsels of God which had remained hidden and unrevealed since the foundation of the world.

### Summary

In these final two public parables Jesus provided consistent predictions about the extended period of time between Israel's rejection of their King and His eventual appearance to establish the kingdom. The fact that there would be a long period of time between these two events was a truth that had not been previously revealed in the Old Testament. An intervening age must come before the millennial kingdom is inaugurated. In all of these public parables Jesus taught that the kingdom will not be established until the end of that age. These parables also illustrated that there would be an uneasy coexistence of good and evil growing side by side throughout this intervening period, so we should not be surprised when we see this during our own lifetime.

# The Private Parables

## (Matthew 13:44-52)

J esus had been teaching while sitting in a boat as the multitude was standing along the shoreline. Then, after He finished sharing four parables publicly with the crowd, he returned to the shore, dismissed the crowd, and went with His disciples back to the house. That is where we will pick up our study of Matt 13 in this chapter.

## Matt 13:36 - Then He left the crowds and went into the house.

Jesus and His disciples entered a setting where He could speak directly and only to them in peace and quiet. His disciples started the conversation by asking Jesus for an explanation of the Parable of the Wheat & Tares, which He immediately gave to them (Matt 13:36-43). Jesus then shared three more "kingdom parables" with His disciples, and finally He concluded by telling them what would be expected of them now that they understood these truths. One Bible commentator introduced this section this way:

> We now turn to the second section of the parables, that is, to those which the King uttered to His disciples alone. Having left the multitudes, His disciples gathered about Him in the quietness of the house. There, first in answer to the request they proffered, He explained to them the parable of the darnel, and then proceeded to give them further instruction. As we turn to the consideration of these parables we must still bear in mind that our Lord is dealing with the subject of the Kingdom in the age between His advents. [Morgan, 131]

So, first Jesus started by telling them the Parable of the Hidden Treasure.

**Matt 13:44 - "The kingdom of heaven is like a treasure hidden in the field, which a man found and hid again; and from joy over it he goes and sells all that he has and buys that field."**

This was another of the unexplained parables which Jesus gave in private only to His disciples. Since Jesus did not explicitly tell us the meaning, we should be cautious as we seek to interpret it. As we did in the last chapter, we will need to look at the biblical context for clues to the meaning of this parable. Remember that, since Jesus gave all of these parables in one sitting, we can be confident that the elements of His overall message were consistent rather than contradictory. As one commentator expressed it, "The figurative terms of these parables are used consistently within the system. That is to say that Jesus was true to His own figures, and used them in one sense only." [Morgan, 34]

There are two familiar elements in this Parable of the Hidden Treasure. First, we see a field and then a man, both of which Jesus already identified for us. The man is the "Son of Man" who is Jesus Himself (v. 37) – and the field is "the world" (v. 38).

One unexplained element is the **treasure**. This is the Greek word *thēsauros* which means "a place in which valuables are kept." It could be thought of as a storehouse or a repository where precious things are stored. As we look through the Bible we see that the word "treasure" is used dozens of times to indicate literal, physical treasure or treasured possessions. However, there are just a few instances where God speaks of something as being His treasure.

For example, Exodus 19:5 says, "Now if you obey me fully and keep my covenant, then out of all nations you will be my treasured possession. Although the whole earth is mine"

Finding the treasure hidden in the field.

(NIV). This uses the Hebrew word *segûllâh* which means "special possession, jewel, or treasure." We see this word again in Deut 26:18 where we read, "The LORD has today declared you to be His people, a treasured possession, as He promised you, and that you should keep all His commandments." The same Hebrew word is used in these six verses where God was speaking of Israel as His treasured possession: Exod 19:5; Deut 7:6; 14:2; 26:18; Ps 135:4; and Mal 3:17. This identification of Israel as the treasure seems to be the most plausible explanation for the subject of this parable. But if the treasure is God's people Israel, then why would they be described as hidden? And why, once the man found them, would they be hidden again? One commentator explained it this way:

When God chose Israel to become His treasure, it was not because they were better than other nations. God wanted a people to represent Him, to be a repository for His Word, and to be an example of what a nation ought to be. God intended Israel to show to the rest of the world how any nation can be blessed with peace and prosperity through a right relationship to Himself. ... In this parable Israel is His treasure. However, when Christ came, Israel was no longer a shining example of what a people in fellowship with God should be. For more than seven hundred years Israel had been the military target of other nations. The people had violated God's laws and become involved in various forms of idolatry. As a result of their backsliding, God allowed them to suffer defeat at the hands of their enemies. When the Lord Jesus Christ appeared in His first advent, His treasure was hidden, that is, the people were scattered without a king. A remnant that returned from their latest captivity was then chafing under the bitter yoke of Rome. God's treasure had failed to fulfill her role. ... He uncovered His treasure, but only for a brief period of time. When they said they would not have Him and openly rejected Him, He hid the treasure again. [Strauss, 92, 93, 94]

The word **hidden** is the Greek word *kruptō* which can mean "kept secret or concealed." This word can also mean something that is typically overlooked. The text says that the treasure was **found**, which is the Greek word *heuriskō*. This can describe something that a person comes across unintentionally, but it can also mean "finding by deliberate enquiry, thought, examination, observation, or detection." Since the Lord Jesus identified Himself as the man in this story, He would have had complete knowledge of all the details concerning the treasure. It might have been hidden from the world's perspective, but nothing can be hidden from God.

This verse says that not only did the man uncover the hidden treasure, but then he hid the treasure again in the field. This is one aspect of the story that seems somewhat surprising. One writer has expressed it this way:

Here perhaps is the touch of greatest mystery in our parable. It affirms the hiding of the treasure discovered. What have we that is parallel to this in the case of Christ? If we think of His ministry and interpret our parable in the light of it, we shall find that this is exactly what He did. He Who called people to the Kingdom of God, because of their refusal, because of their rejection of Him as King, shut the door of the Kingdom and postponed its full realization. By solemn act He rejected the nation, pronounced eight woes over against His eight beatitudes, announced the doom of Jerusalem, flung out the city from the place of government, and postponed for the world the coming of His Kingdom. [Morgan, 143]

So, this might explain why He again hid the treasure in the world. Jesus had come to His people, but Israel had rejected the King and His kingdom. They were unwilling to meet the spiritual requirements for the kingdom's inauguration. Instead they preferred to sink back into their former condition, being scattered and hidden throughout the world, just as they had been for the previous seven hundred years leading up to the birth of their Messiah.

But the story does not end there in this parable. The final phrase says, "from joy over [His treasure] he goes and sells all that he has and buys that field." Jesus did not give up on the unrepentant nation of Israel. They would not accept Him, but He would now do something to prepare the way so He could accept them in the future kingdom.

As for the Lord's **joy** expressed in this verse, the Greek word *chara* means "delight, joy, or rejoicing." There are several biblical examples of God rejoicing over Israel when she is redeemed and restored (Deut 30:9; Isa 62:4-5; 65:19). In Isaiah 65:19 we read, "I will also rejoice in Jerusalem and be glad in My people; And there will no longer be heard in her the voice of weeping and the sound of crying." In that verse the Lord is rejoicing over His people, not as they are in their present condition, but as He knows they will be after He has opened a way for them to enter His future kingdom. In Heb

12:2 we see that Jesus was looking forward with joy to the ultimate result of His atoning death on the cross: "Who for the joy (*chara*) set before Him endured the cross, despising the shame, and has sat down at the right hand of the throne of God."

In this parable, the man's joy over the treasure led him to immediately sell all that he had in order to buy the field. The main emphasis in this parable is the man's extreme act of self-sacrifice in order to obtain the field. The man purchased the field at the cost of everything he had.

When this verse says that the man "**buys** that field" it used the Greek word *agorazō* which is the common word for purchasing something from the marketplace. The people of that day routinely used this term in its straightforward meaning for buying goods or property. This is the sense in which Jesus used the term in this verse – a man bought a field – which pictures a normal transaction after which the man became the sole owner of that property. But as with several other common terms, the writers of the New Testament sometimes invested these words with a special meaning, and *agorazō* is one of those terms. This word was used in specific contexts to describe the redemption of believers which Christ provided through His death on the cross (1 Cor 6:20; 7:23; 2 Pet 2:1; Rev 5:9, 14:3-4). For example, 1 Cor 6:20 says, "For you have been bought with a price: therefore glorify God in your body." And Rev 5:9 says, "And they sang a new song, saying, 'Worthy are You to take the book and to break its seals; for You were slain, and purchased for God with Your blood men from every tribe and tongue and people and nation.'"

The purchase price for the field was the very life of Christ. And notice that Jesus bought, not just the treasure, but the entire field which represents the whole world. So we see that Jesus died to redeem all of the people in all of the world. This seems to be a reference to what theologians call "Unlimited Atonement" (John 1:29; 2 Cor 5:19; 1 Tim 4:10; 1 John 2:2).

For example, when writing to a group of believers the apostle John said, "He Himself is the propitiation for our sins; and not for ours only, but also for those of the whole world" (1 John 2:2). And the apostle Paul wrote to his protégé Timothy, "We have fixed our hope on the living God, who is the Savior of all men, especially of believers" (1 Tim 4:10).

The picture we see in this parable includes one of Jesus' first hints predicting His eventual death. His first explicit statement will soon be given to His disciples in Matt 16:21 which says, "From that time Jesus began to show His disciples that He must go to Jerusalem, and suffer many things from the elders and chief priests and scribes, and be killed, and be raised up on the third day." That statement was later repeated in Matt 17:22-23, then Matt 20:17-19, and finally Matt 26:1-2. But here in this parable, Jesus pictured His death – giving everything in order to purchase the field.

The message of the Parable of the Hidden Treasure springs from Israel's rejection of her King. Even after their rejection of Him, Jesus still treasures them and is willing to sacrifice everything in order to redeem them. As one commentator has said, "The mystery revealed in this parable is the putting aside of Israel's kingdom program for a time. The redemption of the treasure has been accomplished, but the unveiling of it has not." [Toussaint-B, 184] So, at the beginning of the age while the kingdom is postponed, Jesus will purchase His treasured people, but the treasure will remain hidden in the field until the end of the age. One commentator summarized this parable by saying:

> The Lord died for that nation, and still the results of that death are not yet manifested. Israel is hid in the field, in the world. The Lord will come again and return to the field, the world, once more. He comes to claim His inheritance. Then He will lift the treasure, then He will claim His people Israel and they will rejoice in His salvation. During this age, the age of an absent Lord, Israel is kept hid in the field. This is one of the mysteries in the kingdom of the heavens. [Gaebelein, 50-51]

Now Jesus continued by giving His disciples another parable.

**Matt 13:45-46 - "Again, the kingdom of heaven is like a merchant seeking fine pearls, and upon finding one pearl of great value, he went and sold all that he had and bought it."**

There are several familiar elements in this second parable which Jesus shared privately with His disciples. Again, there is a man, which Jesus already identified for us as the "Son of Man" – that is, Jesus Himself. In this parable the man is a **merchant**. This is the Greek word *emporos* which carries the idea of a traveling wholesale dealer, in this case dealing in fine pearls. He is not a common tradesman or a retail shop owner. On the contrary, it seems that he is more important than a simple salesman. His wide experience means that he has seen a lot of different kinds of pearls, so he would be a man who definitely knows quality when he sees it.

At the end of this parable we also see the man selling all that he has in order to buy something precious. So this is another similarity to the Parable of the Hidden Treasure. As one commentator expressed it, "The parables are alike in this, that they both present to us the action of a man who purchases what has value in his eyes at the cost of all he has." [Grant] So in the Parable of the Hidden Treasure we saw that Jesus gave His very life – everything He had – in order to purchase the entire field which represents the whole world. Since these parables communicate a consistent message, we can be confident that here in the Parable of the Pearl again we have a picture of Jesus' act of redemption. We know from the Parable of the Hidden Treasure that in the process of purchasing His people Israel, Jesus also paid the purchase price to redeem the entire world. That parable implied that redemption was available both for believing Jews as well as for believing Gentiles.

"A merchant seeking fine pearls."

The unexplained element in this parable is the "pearl of great value," which is the object that the man purchased or redeemed at the greatest cost. Since the previous parable focused on the redemption of Israel, it seems likely that this parable completed the picture by focusing on the redemption of Gentiles using the metaphor of a pearl. This is a reasonable deduction, but because Jesus did not explain the parable for us, we certainly cannot be dogmatic about this conclusion. Earlier in the Gospels, Jesus did give several hints concerning the salvation of Gentiles (Matt 12:15-21,38-42; Luke 2:30-

32). But this parable would be the only biblical example where the metaphor of a costly pearl was used to represent Gentiles.

While it is true that pearls are not listed as being precious to the Jews, nevertheless the Jews would have understood that pearls were valuable. In Matt 7:6, Jesus warned, "Do not give what is holy to dogs, and do not throw your pearls before swine, or they will trample them under their feet, and turn and tear you to pieces." So, the disciples would have understood the value of pearls. As one commentator explained it,

> These men were, of course, quite conversant with the fact that the pearl was held as a precious stone among the Gentiles. The study of the place of the pearl in Gentile usage is most interesting. From recent investigations made in Egypt, it has been discovered that the decoration of ancient kings consisted largely of gold, inset with jewels, and occasionally with pearls. When we come to Nineveh, we find that the pearl was in greater use. An increasing value was gradually set upon it, until in our day it is accounted as the most precious thing in the East. It is, however, of Gentile value. [Morgan, 159]

So, what we see here is that Jesus used a costly pearl, which was more prized by the Gentiles, as a symbol of something precious for which He would also sacrifice everything. After Israel's rejection of Christ and the postponement of the kingdom, Jesus would do something that the Jews may not have foreseen. Out of joy over His treasure (Israel), He would pay the purchase price, not only for Israel, but also for the Gentiles. As one scholar has said,

> One of the transitions taking place in the text is that Israel, due to its rejection of Christ through its leaders, is being rejected for a time, while Christ does some work that is unexpected, namely the calling out of many unanticipated sons of the kingdom throughout the world. It is not a stretch to see the language of "hiding" to refer to this temporary rejection by Christ. However, the focus of joy by the man in the parable (Christ) shows that He has a heart for the world (the field) in light of the treasure itself. This is in keeping with the theological understanding of the mis-

sion of Israel as a light to the world (e.g., Isaiah 49:6) and the Pauline portrait of Israel's judicial blindness as a boon to the Gentile mission (Rom 11). If this way of taking the passage is valid, it would harmonize well with Matthew's own comprehension of the shift from the focus on Israel to the Gentiles. [Stallard, 355]

So, the message of the Parable of the Pearl is that the redemption which Jesus provided was sufficient, not only for His people Israel, but also for believing Gentiles. At the beginning of the age during which the kingdom is postponed, Jesus will give the ultimate sacrifice to purchase both His treasured people as well as "taking from among the Gentiles a people for His name" (Acts 15:14-18). In the next passage, Jesus will give the final "kingdom parable" privately to His disciples.

**Matt 13:47-48 - "Again, the kingdom of heaven is like a dragnet cast into the sea, and gathering fish of every kind; and when it was filled, they drew it up on the beach; and they sat down and gathered the good fish into containers, but the bad they threw away."**

This parable involves gathering a large number of fish using a dragnet. The Greek word for **dragnet** (*sagēnē*) described a large net that fishermen would drag through the water between two boats. Sometimes they would anchor one end of the net at the shoreline and then drag the net through the water using a single boat. The area of the lake they could cover might be as much as a half mile long, and it would often take a group of men several hours to finish dragging the net onto the beach. A large quantity of fish of all kinds could be gathered using this method. Then the task of sorting the good fish from the bad could begin. The Greek word used here for **bad** is *sapros* which means "of poor quality, unfit for use, or worthless" but it can also mean "rotten or putrefied." For some reason this word picture always reminds me of a very unpleasant odor whenever I imagine that scene. This verse concludes the story, but Jesus continued by sharing the interpretation in the next two verses.

**Matt 13:49-50 - "So it will be at the end of the age; the angels will come forth and take out the wicked from among the righteous, and will throw them into the furnace of fire; in that place there will be weeping and gnashing of teeth."**

Gathering the good fish into containers - throwing the bad fish away.

This explanation sounds similar to that of the Parable of the Wheat & Tares, so it might be helpful to compare these two parables. (See chart on page 98.)

The message of the Parable of the Dragnet is very similar to the Parable of the Wheat & Tares. The Parable of the Wheat & Tares provided more background about how the good and bad seed came to be growing together, while here in the Parable of the Dragnet the emphasis is on the ultimate judgment event that separates the good from the bad. We know that the good and bad will exist side by side throughout the age, but at the time of the gathering, the bad will be cast into the fiery furnace.

As we mentioned with the Parable of the Wheat & Tares, this judgment is reminiscent of the "Judgment of the Sheep & Goats" which we read about in Matt 25:31-46. The sheep, the wheat, and the good fish will inherit the kingdom, while the goats, the tares, and the bad fish will be judged. This will occur after the future seven-year Tribulation, and it is a judgment of its living survivors. "When the Son of Man comes in His glory, and all the angels with Him, then He will sit on His glorious throne. All the nations will be gathered before Him; and He will separate them from one another, as the shepherd separates the sheep from the goats." (Matt 25:31-32)

This might also be a good place to look at the relationship between the parables in this chapter. (See diagram on page 99). The Parable of the Sower introduced the six "kingdom parables" which follow, and then the Parable of the Householder concluded the series with additional admonitions from Jesus. The first three "kingdom parables" were given publically to the multitude, and Jesus did not explain any of those parables for the crowd. The Parable of the Wheat & Tares is a fairly long story, and Jesus explained that parable later only for His disciples. The next two public parables, the Parable of the Mustard Seed and the Parable of the Leaven, were quite short, and Jesus did not give an explanation for either of

| Events | Wheat & Tares | the Dragnet |
|---|---|---|
| Good and evil grow side by side | v38 - the good seed, these are the sons of the kingdom; and the tares are the sons of the evil one | v47 - a dragnet cast into the sea, and gathering fish of every kind (good & bad) |
| Separation of good from evil | v30 - in the time of the harvest I will say to the reapers, "First gather up the tares and bind them in bundles to burn them up; but gather the wheat into my barn." | v48 - and when it was filled, they drew it up on the beach; and they sat down and gathered the good fish into containers, but the bad they threw away. |
| End of the Age: Gathering of the wicked | v40 - So shall it be at the end of the age.<br>v41 - Son of Man will send forth His angels, and they will gather out of His kingdom all stumbling blocks, and those who commit lawlessness | v49 - So it will be at the end of the age; the angels will come forth and take out the wicked from among the righteous |
| Judgment of the wicked | v42 - and will throw them into the furnace of fire; in that place there will be weeping and gnashing of teeth. | v50 - and will throw them into the furnace of fire; in that place there will be weeping and gnashing of teeth. |
| Righteous enter the kingdom | v43 - Then THE RIGHTEOUS WILL SHINE FORTH AS THE SUN in the kingdom of their Father. | (not mentioned) |

**Sower** (Introductory parable)

    **Wheat & Tares**

      **Mustard Seed + Leaven**

*Public Parables:* spoken to the crowd

    **Hidden Treasure + Pearl**

  **Dragnet** *(Good & Bad Fish)*

**Householder** (Concluding parable)

*Private Parables:* spoken to the disciples

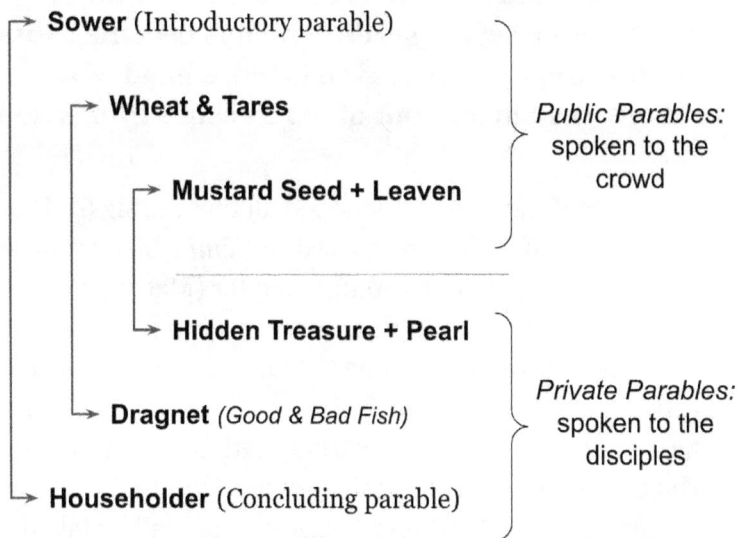

them. After entering the house with His disciples, Jesus gave another pair of very brief parables, again without explanation. The last "kingdom parable", the Parable of the Dragnet, was a story with clear parallels to the Parable of the Wheat & Tares. As one commentator has said,

> The kingdom parables can be divided into three couplets. ... These six parables are all introduced with the phrase "the kingdom of heaven is like." The whole picture presented relates some truth connected with the kingdom of heaven. The two parables not yet discussed (the parable of the sower and the parable of things old and new) omit this introductory phrase. These form the introduction and conclusion to these three couplets of kingdom parables. [Benson, 6]

So now Jesus will conclude His private discussion with His disciples by asking a question and, based on their response, He will give them one final parable in this series.

**Matt 13:51-52 - "Have you understood all these things?" They said to Him, "Yes." And Jesus said to them, "Therefore every scribe who has become a disciple of the kingdom of heaven is like a head of a household, who brings out of his treasure things new and old."**

Jesus asked, "Have you understood all these things?" The word **understood** is the Greek word *suniēmi* which we have seen several times previously in this chapter (Matt 13:13-15, 19, 23). It means "to put together mentally or to comprehend," and it involves assembling the facts into an organized whole, like collecting all of the pieces of a jigsaw puzzle and putting them together. We know from Matt 13:12 that to the one who understands "more shall be given," but to the one who refuses to understand "even what he has shall be taken away from him." The disciples respond by saying that they did understand, so Jesus says, "Therefore" – because they understood – He is able to share this final parable which emphasizes their new responsibilities in light of their understanding of these kingdom truths.

In this final parable Jesus used the word **scribe**, which is the Greek word *grammateus*. This word had a rather negative connotation because of the evil behavior of the scribes and Pharisees who opposed Jesus. But the word itself simply means someone who is familiar with the Word of God and is able to correctly interpret it while teaching others. We can be confident that this original meaning is the one intended here because of how this person is described in the following phrase. Jesus says this is a scribe who has become a "disciple of the kingdom of heaven." The word **disciple** is the Greek word *mathēteuō* which means "to become a learner, student, or dedicated follower of one's teacher." So here the phrase "become a disciple of the kingdom of heaven" indicates someone who has been taught the "mysteries of the kingdom of heaven" which Jesus has shared throughout this chapter.

Why didn't Jesus leave out the word scribe and simply say that a "disciple of the kingdom of heaven" is like a householder? It may be because the responsibility of a disciple is to learn, but the responsibility of a scribe is to teach the truths they have learned.

Jesus says that this learner/teacher "is like a head of a household." The phrase **head of a household** is the single Greek word *oikodespotēs* which means the leader, the master, or the final authority in the household. This is a person in a position of responsibility over everything within his domain. By using this term, Jesus is conferring on the disciples some new responsibilities. Not only are they to learn and understand, but they are also to write, to teach, and to oversee the correct interpretation of these kingdom truths.

The householder is responsible for administering the "treasure" or resources of his house. Jesus said that he "brings out of his treasure things new and old." So, in the same way that a householder carries out his responsibilities, Jesus' disciples now have the task of putting together and teaching the old as well as the new truths that they have been given. One commentator expressed it this way: "These parables set forth the prophecies and history of the kingdom between the two advents of the King. ... Our Lord had taught them in the parables what could be expected during His absence and until He returns." [Strauss, 125]

Another scholar has said,

This parable teaches that these new kingdom mysteries as disclosed in the parables found in Matthew 13 must be considered alongside Old Testament kingdom truth if one is to understand the totality of God's kingdom agenda. ... Only by augmenting these new inter-advent teachings found in Matthew 13 alongside what they already knew about the kingdom from the Old Testament would they be able to understand all that God is doing and will do. [Woods, 134]

As we end this series on the parables of Matthew 13, we should remember that we are living during that inter-advent age today, and since we have been taught the truths of the kingdom, then we also have a responsibility to share these truths with others.

# Conclusion

**That day Jesus went out of the house and was sitting by the sea (Matt 13:1).**

As we come to the conclusion of that "busy day" which ended with Jesus sharing the eight parables in Matthew chapter thirteen, we should reflect on what we have learned from our study of His work and words.

Jesus had been offering His kingdom to the nation of Israel by proclaiming to His people, "Repent, for the kingdom of heaven is at hand" (Matt 4:17). This kingdom was the same one that God had promised throughout the Old Testament and which the Jews had been anticipating for hundreds of years. Nearly every Old Testament prophet had spoken of the future restoration of the kingdom and the fulfillment of God's covenants with the nation of Israel.

But their restoration came with conditions. Deuteronomy 17:15 stated, "You shall surely set a king over you whom the LORD your God chooses, one from among your countrymen you shall set as king over yourselves." Jesus was (and is) God's chosen King who presented Himself to the nation and held out the offer of establishing the long-awaited kingdom. Not only must Israel recognize Jesus as the King chosen by God, but they must also meet the spiritual condition of national repentance and personal holiness that was clearly stated in their Scriptures (e.g., Lev 11:45; 1 Kings 8:47; Ezek 18:29-32). At that pivotal time in their history, when the nation of Israel could have seen the inauguration of their kingdom, they were quite unwilling to meet its requirements.

Instead, their leaders opposed the message and ministry of their King and eventually signed His death warrant.

During the brief time of ministry remaining to Him, Jesus focused on teaching His individual followers rather than on preaching to the nation. Near the end of His time on earth He would declare, "For I say to you, from now on you will not see Me until you say, 'BLESSED IS HE WHO COMES IN THE NAME OF THE LORD!'" (Matt 23:39) What we see in the parables of Matthew 13 are prophetic glimpses into the characteristics of the time during which the kingdom is postponed. The kingdom would not come for Israel until the end of this intervening age.

The parables revealed some of the secret plans of God – things which had not been revealed in the Old Testament. As Jesus said in Matt 13:11, "To you it has been granted to know the mysteries of the kingdom of heaven, but to them it has not been granted." These truths were given to the individuals who would believe in Jesus as the Messiah and who expressed their willingness to repent and pursue the righteousness that was required of members of the future kingdom – a righteousness which comes by faith.

We saw that Jesus told the introductory Parable of the Sower to illustrate several of the reasons why the multitude in Israel had not responded to the word of the kingdom. Some were completely hardened and hostile to the message: their hearts had become insensitive, their ears barely heard, and they deliberately closed their eyes and refused to understand. Others seemed enthusiastically receptive at first, but their unwillingness to put their complete trust in Jesus led them to fall away under the external pressures of affliction and persecution. Still others became distracted from the truth by the cares of this life and the pursuit of material gain. These responses illustrated why the multitude within Israel had not eagerly accepted their King. We should understand that these same hindrances are still active today and that they will deter many from understanding the truth.

The message of the Parable of the Wheat & Tares is that there is an active enemy of Christ at work in the world. One of his strategies is to create counterfeits of the truth which are intended to deceive people and to divert them from devotion to Jesus. Because of this enemy activity, we will see good and evil growing side by side throughout the course of this age. But we have the Lord's assurance that the separation will come and justice will be done at the end of the age. "The righteous WILL shine forth as the sun in the kingdom of their Father" (Matt 13:43).

The Parable of the Mustard Seed augmented the message of the Parable of the Wheat & Tares. The kingdom would not come until the time of harvest at the end of the age. Jesus illustrated this truth using a tiny seed which was familiar to His audience, that when fully grown became a small tree where the birds could perch and where they could feed on the seed pods which had become ripe for the harvest. When we see the gathering birds and the ripe pods on the mustard tree, we know that the time for the kingdom to be established is near at hand.

The Parable of the Leaven pictures a corrupting influence which spreads through the dough over time, and this also amplifies one of the messages of the Parable of the Wheat & Tares. Evil will eventually dominate the age before the coming kingdom. But after evil has run its course, there will be a judgment event followed by the establishment of the kingdom by the glorified King.

In the Parable of the Hidden Treasure we see that the treasure was hidden, then uncovered briefly, then hidden again, and finally purchased along with the entire field. This pictures the condition of the nation of Israel at the time of Jesus. They were (and are) scattered and hidden throughout the world. When Jesus came, He uncovered Israel and proclaimed to them the word of the kingdom. But upon their rejection of their King, He covered them again until a future time when He would return and lift the treasure. In the meantime, Jesus went to the cross to pay the ultimate price, not only for His treasure Israel, but for the entire world as well. The Parable of the Pearl illustrates the truth that Jesus gave the ultimate sacrifice to purchase both His treasured people as well as "taking from among the Gentiles a people for His name" (Acts 15:14-18).

The message of the final kingdom parable, the Parable of the Dragnet, is parallel to that of the Parable of the Wheat & Tares. There we learned that good and evil will exist side by side throughout this age, but at the culmination of the age the bad will be cast into the fiery furnace. The Parable of the Dragnet emphasized the ultimate judgment event that separates the good from the bad.

In the Parable of the Householder Jesus shared that, because His disciples now understand these new mysteries of the kingdom, they are responsible for putting them together with the Old Testament revelation about the kingdom in order to form a comprehensive whole. And beyond that, they are now responsible for teaching these combined truths of the kingdom to others who are eager to understand and follow Jesus. At the end of another of Jesus' parables He told His listeners to apply the truths of its message. He said, "You go, and do likewise" (Luke 10:37). Let all of us now go and apply the truths we have been taught by sharing them with others who desire to learn.